A Child of the Air

By the same author

Non-fiction
Angels
Invocations
The Arts of Life
Inner Beauty
Inner Space
Padma's Story
Madhuban
The Poetry of Teaching

Fiction
Fire-fly
Sleeping with Mozart
Liftman

A Child of the Air

Anthea Church

Shakspeare EDITORIAL

First published in the UK in 2025 by Shakspeare Editorial, UK

Copyright © 2025 Anthea Church

www.antheachurch.co.uk

ISBN 978-1-7384422-0-1 (paperback)
ISBN 978-1-7384422-1-8 (ebook)

All rights reserved. No part of this publication may be reproduced or used in any manner without written permission from the publisher.

The moral rights of the author have been asserted.

Cover design #andydixon64
Typesetting www.ShakspeareEditorial.org

All incidents in this book are factual. To the best of her ability, the author has attempted to tell the truth throughout. However, to avoid giving pain to anyone featured, some names have been changed.

For Susie Griffin

Maybe all that a family is, is the stories we do not tell. Maybe all that a family is, is the shape of its silence. For there in that silence lies all the family's shame, and all of its values, and all of its most desperate longings. Often, in the vault of a family's untold stories are the most important things.

Kei Miller, from *Things I Have Withheld*

CONTENTS

Preface	xi
24 January 1958	1
The Boarder	14
'The Lunatics' (1)	27
The Materialist	36
The Patient	48
The Non-Academic	60
The Adolescent	73
The Ingenue	84
Recovery	97
The Follower	106
'The Lunatics' (2)	127
The Seeker	135
The Drifter	150
Last Steps	153

PREFACE

In her early twenties, Anthea Church's privileged middle-class life appeared to veer dramatically off course when she joined an Indian cult. This memoir, the first of a trilogy, tells of the years that led up to that decision.

The book could have been written in a thousand different ways but what emerges is a picture of a child who blithely accepted whatever came her way. She was brought up not to ask questions, not to complain, just to get on with it. The negligence that becomes apparent in many of the incidents described, while not an indication of love withheld, sets the book firmly in an era when parents of a certain social class tended to pitch their offspring into the world without so much as a word of warning. At the age of three, being picked up by a random lorry driver and taken for a ride around her childhood village seemed to provoke little consternation. The same went for a collision with nudity and sex during a French exchange. No letters of complaint were written to the school responsible for the experience, no questions asked either by the child or her parents. When she ends up in love with a mystic who suggests that in a previous life she was a disciple, she receives the information with neither pride nor disbelief.

Now in her sixties, Anthea feels that it is the right time to conduct an examination of three very different stages of her life. She asserts that much of what she tells will be unknown even to her siblings and closest friends but hopes that they can now share with her the joys, the fears and the sorrows of that previously hidden life

Anthea Church is an accomplished and versatile writer. She has over fifteen publications to her name, from the contemplative to the romantic, from the humorous to the tragic. This trilogy, the telling of her extraordinary personal story, will embrace all these different voices. I commend this highly readable first memoir of that trilogy to any reader with a love of entertainment and a fascination with childhood.

Ian Anderson
Friend and Coach

24 JANUARY 1958

My father was out with his gun shooting god knows what. When he arrived in the maternity ward, my mother had her own ammunition: Where the hell had he been? Had he forgotten that the baby was expected to career down the birth canal at any moment? Why did he never think...?

This sort of accusation was fired at him frequently during their long and happy marriage, and even more often at their newly-born third child. From the beginning, my habits were every bit as evasive and blithe as his were. One part of me resisted life in the world, longing instead to loll in the warmth of amniotic fluid; another wanted constantly to interrogate life, and find out more about my oldest brother, Andrew, who died before he had experienced a full month in this world.

There should have been four of us. Though perhaps I would not have been thought of, if Andrew had survived. His grave is still there in the tiny Somerset village of Cossington. Nobody weeds it.

Let us, as they say, park the sadness of that loss and focus on me: the Evader.

Danger was the state I got my kicks from. Always hopping, always rushing, heading for a fall...

So did I fall?

My parents thought so, certainly.

Take for a start, my crawl. Not as most children, across grass or carpet, or like my sister, who bumped and jumped on her backside. I tended rather to steer myself up steps, onto the lower branches of trees, the rim of a stone urn, along an uneven wall, the roof of a rabbit hutch... My addiction to climbing has lasted a lifetime. Not up any of the world's ladders, but away from the earth.

At the age of twenty-two, making evasion my vocation, I removed myself to a nunnery.

'Why?'

'Come on! Why a nunnery?'

'I had no choice.'

'How come?'

I cannot answer big questions on demand, nor unpack the epiphany that led not even to a cloister, but...

'An *Eastern* nun?'

'Something like that.'

Leave aside the epiphany. Maybe the answer has to do with being contained. As a teacher, I have spoken warmly about the importance of freedom, just as I have encouraged students to hurdle over clichés in order to find their own best words in their own best order.

But perhaps freedom has only ever interested me as an idea. Imprisonment is more to my taste – for that means an institution to escape from, a wall to hit my head against, an enemy to sharpen my wits on. Another evasion. Battle relieves me of facing the blank of the day. Or myself. I am too much. For others, for my former husband, for bosses who would tame my off-grid style of teaching, for myself...

Happiness is to be found only in the anticipation of those few moments of grace after the battle is over.

All of it over.

Robert Frost wrote that 'the best way out is through'. I respect but do not enjoy *through-ing*. I want *out*. Get out of it fast, escape, wander off...

And not from any particular it, but from life itself.

There.

It is said.

Still small, I found myself one morning on the roof of the family's clapped-out Land Rover, parked on the gravelled driveway of our Devon farmhouse. I pressed my tummy against khaki canvas, as the sun warmed my back. A fearful visitor called my mother from a flowerbed. Again and again, I am dragged down to the safety of the grass.

Another bored morning, I stretched up to open the green gates that divided house from village and wandered into the road. A moment later, spade-shaped hands lifted me high in the air onto the grey-pebbled seat of a lorry. Beside me, a driver with a face smudged by soil and no smile. At last! The prospect of a ride round the village in the company of a murderer.

Our circular route took in the Lotus Pottery. After that, the War Memorial, the sweet shop, the post office, the Co-op— forbidden for being run by *those ruddy socialists* (my father) — up past the butcher's, the newsagent's. Finally, around the corner to the primary school, where I would soon spend three happy years pressing wax crayons onto cheap, crimson sugar paper.

The last leg was a trip along a road adjacent to the orchard, an extension of the family garden. Then the driver closed the circle and slithered back down the hill to the gate that opened onto the paradise of that long, white Devon house: Yarde – home and refuge.

How I scrambled down from the high-chair of his lorry, what my chauffeur said of our jaunt around the village, and whether his motive was rescue or abduction, I shall never know. Only the scrunch of my mother's feet across the gravel is still audible to me, as well as memory of a smack then a question.

'Did anything happen?'

What could 'anything' refer to? The view of the village on high? The sight of my own hands folded in my lap? The driver's face? It doesn't matter, for my unrumpled clothing sufficed to ease my mother back to the sanctuary of her flowerbed.

Later, all three Church children would yearn to escape the long low farmhouse that is Yarde. Its peace and quiet would oppress them. The River Dart and the freshness of the Devon air were delightful, but nothing of interest happened in Stoke Gabriel. That was also why it was such a fine home, for the outside world would have plenty of shocks to meeken them.

As an adult, I now see that those who evade are generally liars. I do have a tendency to lie. It's quicker for a start.

One childhood fabrication involved a dream whose villain was a version of the lorry driver. When he first turned up to interrupt my night, he was friendly enough, a stocking over his head to contour the pleasing bulge of his nose. He even offered me a Ginger Nut – my brother's favourite booty from the biscuit tin before breakfast.

Elaboration followed for as long as the dream could carry conviction. The stocking became a bottle of washing-up liquid. A squirt of poison landed in my eye. Finally, the poison was emitted not from the bottle but the barrel of a gun fixed to the bottle with Binder Twine. Perhaps the gun was my father's?

I am blinded.

Having learnt how to win the kind of tactile response I yearned for, I embellished the gun dream at least once a month. For the rewards might then include longer spells in my parents' bed, an extra cup of hot milk, or more time listening to the dulcet morning radio tones of the inebriated Jack de Manio. My mother had a thing for Jack de Manio – even though it was he who brought news that Marilyn Monroe had committed suicide, Nelson Mandela had been arrested and, on her small child's birthday, a B-52 carrying two hydrogen bombs had crashed on a farm in Faro, North Carolina.

I have never dropped the behaviours which lead to gaining attention. Reliable sources plague us with the truth that methods used in childhood are those most often carried into adult life. Perhaps it was a reaction against this pride-destroying tendency that led me in the end to seek out the attention of God. Talking to God would release me from the shame of bothering anyone else, and would thus rack up a notch of that precious commodity: self-respect. In stricter moods, I know this is another evasion, for we can always pretend we are talking to God when we may just as well be talking to ourselves.

My first version of God, as it seems to be for many arty types, was my primary school teacher, a woman of severity whose attention I sought with demented enthusiasm. Daily, I arrived early in Mrs Johnson's Nissen hut where she perched in a pink overall on the top rung of a ladder. Or was Mrs Johnson in fact only once perched on a ladder? Perhaps it was the time I presented her with a story she must read *now this minute.*

As a teacher myself, I know only too well the pain of being asked to peruse a child's stories. It's worse when they proffer a novella which they'd like me to edit *but don't change it; I like it as it is.*

I can remember only that Mrs Johnson wasn't much interested. And this hurt my feelings, as it did when my first school report described me as bossy. The sound of the word repulsed me as much as the fat shape it made on the page. I reacted by shape-shifting to the size of a doll and climbing into my cot for a sleep.

Sleep has always been my answer to distress, much as it is for Arthur Miller's nasty little anti-hero, Joe Keller. But, at three, I experienced strange sensations on waking, many a morning opening my eyes to feel limbs swelling and buzzing so loudly that they seemed to fill the entire house: arms fat, legs as long as the village. Only when someone entered the room did the sensation stop, as if a balloon had been pricked and I was returned to my ordinary size, shape, being.

Not long after joining Mrs Johnson's class, I took up the mystical hobby of ballet, an art that epitomised all that was lovely. Twice weekly, I would stand in a chilly studio in Paignton, a coastal town of extreme sluggishness, stretching and pointing, pointing and stretching, as often as possible on one leg. I liked also to be positioned in the front row, my gaze cast longingly at the instructor – an exotic Miss Pamela de Vaal whose elongated feet, as she went from first, to second, to third positions, were reflected in the mirror to make an infinity of Modiglianis.

Halfway through the class, we would switch to galloping – an inferior activity. But the sensation of free movement brought blessed relief for one who was more like a wild horse on a beach than an eventing steed, plaited and ribboned for dressage.

After galloping came a return to pointing and stretching, pointing and stretching until sluggish Paignton could be stretched no more and my mother turned up, cradling a bowl of stew, wrapped in pages of *The Telegraph*, to be eaten in the passenger seat of the family's old Wolseley.

One day Miss de Vaal called me to a small room at the back of the studio, pointed to a chair, and asked if I would like to take part in a ballet competition.

'Yes.'

'Yes *please*.'

'Yes-please-thank-you.'

I cannot recall the dance to be performed in a hall in Torquay – another town of extraordinary dullness. But it was practised each evening in front of my father, who was doubtless as bored as Mrs Johnson had been. I needed him to watch. Even when he made those habitual long groaning noises, I delighted in his presence.

A couple of weeks before the competition, Miss de Vaal summoned me back to the small room, pointed to the chair and said: 'We'd like you to wear a tutu.' My legs – brought up on hand-me-down shorts and aertex – began swinging at high speed.

'Stop it!'

The evening before the competition, I practised with the speed that only child or manic can summon. My dream that night has resisted editing ever since. About to begin my routine, I found myself on a hybrid of forklift, scaffolding platform and crane. As I pointed and stretched, jumped and skipped, the platform rose slowly into the air, becoming smaller and smaller until we were the size of a pinhead.

Somewhere in an old blue album is a black and white snap, taken next morning, of a child in a tutu, kneeling on a stout leg, arms in first position, fine brown hair scraped back into a bun with a spray of Elnette, bearable in its stink only thanks to an enticing gold container.

My main rival was a talented thug called Jacky Collins. She lived in the council houses, those places of mystery reserved for *people of inferior breeding*. How embarrassing it is to be dogged by snobbishness – even though I kicked so aggressively against it in my teens.

Jacky was first onto the stage, while I sat in the front row, the rough gauzy tutu making my thighs itch. I cheered myself by looking down at the pink sheen of ribbon that criss-crossed my legs from ankle to knee. Now and then I stole a vicious glance at my competitor's routine which was, I thought, carried out in a cavalier fashion.

When it was my turn, oblivious to the fact that the music was yet to begin, my body set off at such speed that I finished half way through the music – delighted to have beaten the pianist. But the result meant a long time standing alone on stage, first in the far corner, then centre… I gawped at the audience, the judges, my feet, the wings… Suddenly a voice shouted 'SMILE!' – and the ordeal was over.

Timing has always posed problems. On another occasion, when I was four and at school, Mrs Johnson was plinking out a tune on the piano while the class had to hold hands and dance in a circle. Perhaps it was the dislike of hand-holding, or hearing between the notes Mrs Johnson's disapproval of my uppity breeding, but I made a mistake. Mrs Johnson pounced, took a ruler from her pocket and delivered a sharp whack to my shins. I wet my pants. Then walked up School Hill at the end of the day in such shame that I revealed nothing of the mishap. Once home, I ran upstairs, ripped off my knickers, scrunched them into a ball, hid them inside a pair of my brother's shorts, and flung them into the square white washing box in the corner of his bedroom. I had disappointed Mrs Johnson, deceived my mother and made a fool of myself. I no longer wet my pants, but it troubles me that I make other such mistakes to this day.

Back at the ballet competition, a group of women bossed each other up onto the stage and took their seats behind a trestle table. The audience could enjoy an untrammelled view of their grown-up legs, crossed and solid in bunioned walking shoes. When the winner was announced, Jacky Collins was in first place, others second, third and fourth, and *you last*. My mother turned to me and chirruped: 'So that's the end of ballet.' These days, a mother wouldn't admit to their daughter that they lacked talent. They'd email the adjudicator to demand reasons why their daughter hadn't won, was criticised, or offered only lukewarm praise. And then the recriminations: She's devastated, will never recover, is scarred for life. And the reparations: I would ask you please to apologise, give her at least one complementary (and complimentary) lesson, tell her how wonderful she really is…

In contrast, my parents were quite happy to advertise to the world the cluelessness of their children, for we were as much victims of their humorous disapproval as those who lived in council houses, or people who were too dressy.

Perhaps because of my mother, Mrs Johnson, Miss Pamela de Vaal and the women who misjudged my dancing, I had a thing for females in authority, as long as they were a) experts, b) kind, c) enjoyed at least one distinguishing visual feature.

Brown Owl qualified on all counts. Wherever she was spotted – in church, the village shop, the parish hall, running her Brownie pack, or in my head where I pictured her wearing rubber gloves and standing at a sink in a kitchen in a house at the top of a steep, intriguing drive – it was her teeth that were so fascinating. For being buck, and so permanently rammed down on her bottom lip, they produced a pleasing little spittle ball at each corner of her mouth. Perhaps because she couldn't breathe with her mouth closed, Brown Owl's voice had a nasal quality which created an unexpectedly wide space into which I mentally placed stationery, cake, pink nightdresses, and other up-cheering items which, for some reason, I associated with her.

Like my two aunts and first cousin, Brown Owl had no visible ankles. Her shins seemed to spill over the edge of their flat brown shoes, which themselves resembled the conkers my brother and I played with beneath the chestnut tree in Yarde's driveway.

Brown Owl's daughter was in my class. Born prematurely (*they brought her home in a shoebox* – my mother), she sported, at the age of five, a set of baby dentures. Aware of this fact and indifferent to her problem, I used her as the scapegoat to distance myself from the pain perpetrated by the hard-nosed little classmates who hated my poshness and shoved and pushed and hurled unkind words, sometimes stones, in my direction as I plodded up School Hill in the direction of Yarde.

One day, particularly upset by an episode of taunting, I happened upon Brown Owl's daughter hanging upside down from a low bar in the playground, ponytail dangling towards the thick, cheese-rubbery mat beneath.

Her mouth was wide open in wonder at seeing the world upside down, and her false teeth suddenly flew from her gums. Promptly, I claimed them, shoved them into my knickers, walked curt in my ironed frock, and shoved the teeth between the slats of the drain at the bottom of the steps that led up to our Nissen hut classroom. I felt no guilt about this act of downright cruelty – it seemed exactly the right thing to do. I certainly didn't consider the effect of my unkindness upon Brown Owl, for I was never in the habit of linking one person with another. Mummy was Mummy, Daddy Daddy, Brown Owl Brown Owl; each entire unto themselves, and each capable of recovering in isolation from the cruelties inflicted on their kin. As for how much it might cost Brown Owl to purchase another set of dentures for the tiny pink mouth of her child, I thought nothing of it. My innocent world was funded not by money, but by love.

A few days later, I was in the parish hall, holy and excited, finally to be sworn in as a Brownie. Everything was ready: stones laid out to make a winding path, toadstools, a badge or two on a table, and all attendees hushed in anticipation. There followed the Brownie salute – a sort of sideways Nazi gesture – and then the assignment to a six (aka team). Mine was the Gnomes – a puny let-down of a name.

From that day on, I could wear the brown uniform, a garment that reeked of unappealing, outdoor activities. My mother sat in the lamplight and sewed on the badge, with its small squiggle that looked like a bleached tadpole. I fiddled about with pieces of paper brought by Brown Owl, who also ran Sunday School.

As an adult, I would return to the Brownie Hall for coffee mornings with my elderly mother, who liked to talk. Down the hill to the hall we would go, in order to inspect the stalls: 'Very nice cake. How good. How's your daughter? How's your Derek? Oh, I am sorry. Oh well, not to worry. That's a nice piece of needlework.' All this, followed by a bellowing fanged laugh – for my mother had a rogue, pointed molar which provoked in my father a kind of breathless laughing fit that was infectious.

After his funeral, we went to the same hall for the wake, which should surely be called the sleep, where I sat at a trestle table and cried. Not among relations; they were as English and above tears as I had been, both as child and nun. I cried with two women from the village who had taken it in turns to clean my parents' bungalow in their later years, and who could howl like babies, as could I.

For by that time I was broken. And glad of it.

THE BOARDER

At eight, torn from primary school, Yarde, Mrs Johnson, the Brownies, my siblings, the biscuit tin, the urns, the well, the lawn, my parents, I was sent to a small boarding school in East Devon. It housed twenty-six children, all girls but for one – Jonathan, who, with his shoulder-length hair and damp hands, perhaps thought he was a girl too, as we did.

My sister, four years older, had been there too, but had now been shunted on to its senior school, Shute – an apt name for the horrors it inflicted. The more unhappy my sister is, the quieter she becomes. My response to sorrow is to put on an obnoxious show of cheerfulness. In a letter to my mother, the headmistress of Pippins wrote: 'your daughter never stopped talking from the moment she got into the car to the moment we returned to school.'

And in letters I write with volubility, already adopting the mask I am to wear for the rest of my life.

Pippins
Axminster
Devon

19 November 1966

Dear Mummy and Daddy

Thank you for all your letters. Today I am going to Miss Tongs. I am going this after noon. I have got another stinking cold. I have been in bed for two days. Its awfully boaring in this classroom. So I have started my letter and pritended it is ruff. We are still playing games at night, and it is good fun, last night because there was only four of us instead of seven. The head of our dormy was away and two others. By the way I couldn't go out with Susan Quinland. Because Mip said her mother was to busy. We are still having arithmetic. But it is easy. Mummy PLEASE will you send me an Advent calendar. Mummy I have found out I have to get more presents for Sherilyn and others. Miss Young just said it is real letter writing. So I can write another letter. Blacky and Tabby are very well.

Sunday

Yesterday I went to Miss Tongs for tea. Anna, Maryann and I went. We had a supper time. For tea we had sticky buns, chocalate biscuits and sandwiches. After that we watched television. I am glad I went because I missed a long walk and also we went to a fair. Each of us bought a twopenny cake and a candle holder for Mip. She was very pleased. Then Mip payed 6d for us to play a game. You see you had to get 25 marbles into a flower pot with a fork. Last night I had some sparklers to share out. I expect you wonder where I got them. Well I swopped them with Sara for some ... that I had read. It was super fun. Because Mip turned all the lights out.

Much love Anthea your daughter.

Pippins
Axminster

Dear Mummy and Daddy

I hope you are well. I am having a lovely time at school. I am much better. Give my love to Mummy when she comes back Daddy I wonder if Mummy will meet Auntie Phillipa. I am dying for half term and for Mummy to send Patch and some, clothes. I have not got any clothes for her. Any way today I got up to fifth branch on Old Firry but could not get on to it. I cryed a little and materon had to get me down. I like Dancing very much. Also I like music very very very much. I can do two hands easily now. I love, it. This afternoon we are going for a picnic. I don't know, where to. Will you give my love to the animals. Also Auntie Phillipa and the Thomas family.

Sunday

Yesterday we went for a long LONG LONG walk. Doyin pushed Poochy in her pram. It was a walk and a bicycle walk. But you see I hadn't got one. So next term or even better after half term. Any way when we got back I was EXHAUSTED. Last night we were aloud to come down. We saw Batman and the beggining of the mountain.

Today we went to church. When we came out.

We had another walk. But it wasn't quite so long. Yesterday when we came back from our walk we played cafeas. The people who were not running the cafe were not aloud in Miss Banks form. Any way we had good fun. I have got a surprise to tell you. We have got kittens at Pippins. One is called Tabatha and the other is called Sooty. They are sweet. When I had just been ill I wasn't aloud in Miss Banks form room. Because it was too cold. So I sat in Mips room. Then Mip said Bring up the kittens. So I did. NOTHING MORE TO SAY.

I was at the school for only two years, but Pippins takes up a disproportionate space in my psyche. It isn't a static memory, but unfolds like frames of a film that can last the length of a night.

I was in many ways happy there.

Last summer, I returned to Pippins. It looked the same – a square Georgian house with flaking paintwork surrounded by fields. Only Old Firry had gone. This was the affectionate name given to a large conifer in the garden. Whenever boarders were dropped off at the end of the holidays, it was to this tree they went, clinging to its trunk and staring up longingly at its height.

When small girls join the school from which I have just retired, I always suggest that they wander into the grounds and find a tree to adopt. Later in the term, when they are becoming fractious, I despatch them back to their trees.

Old Firry was not merely a source of consolation but a

challenge, for it was headline-grabbing if you could climb to the top and wave to your friends below. I was keen to be in on this achievement, because life was a competition. And height was a bed in the sky.

Jumbled up with Old Firry comes the memory of a pupil with a wide smile and tombstone teeth, who has now merged with a rather unpleasant student I taught about fifteen years ago, who disliked my informal manner of teaching. In the same instinctively negative way, this girl – let's call her Yolanda – took against me. So I was filled with relief when she went absent with measles. But Yolanda soon returned and, just at the point when I was ready to climb Old Firry, in dictatorial manner she appointed herself as guide, no one being permitted to brave the climb alone.

On the set day, the entire school gathered at the foot of old Firry. Matron, to the fore, prepared for the worst: that either I or Yolanda might tumble from on high into her arms, and from there into plaster. Yolanda led the way, robust, freckled and competent.

There was a particular route through the branches, and a fixed method of climbing. Yolanda would make a move, then wait. I would copy, and so it would continue in a climb rich with the fragrance of pine, the sensation of rough bark against child skin, and sporadic glimpses of sky through branches. The last few branches were difficult, in the way the last part of many undertakings tends to be difficult. As we reached the tiny top branch, a cheer sounded, like the whoosh of the sea in a shell held to the ear. Then a roar as Yolanda and I performed the last and most dangerous manoeuvre, which was to tie a handkerchief to the top branch, thus adding to the twenty or so other white cotton squares that could sometimes be seen, fluttering on a summer evening from the scrunch of the school driveway.

The name of the school was Pippins. Its owner was Mip. Her twin sister, Pip, was second in command. Their real names were a secret – not even our parents seemed to know, though they must have written sizeable cheques to the P&M bank account. Whoever they were, both seemed to be in their eighties. They had immobile white perms and have now joined forces in my mind with the Mother Superior in *The Sound of Music*. The Church children watched that film on the same evening that our grandmother lay unconscious under a table in a cottage in Plymtree, which was occupied by thirty real pugs, and as many in porcelain.

Mip and Pip were involved with the Women's Institute, which is probably where the idea of Pippins was mooted. My mother was in charge of the Devon branch, nicknamed the Twitters by my father, because they never stopped talking, especially on the telephone, a gadget he loathed.

Mip was severe but kind, though many of her habits might seem questionable to the government inspectors who stifle the flourishing of adventure among the young of today. Each morning, she would summon five of her smallest pupils to her bedroom – a small box just outside their dormitory. There they would kneel beside her bed, not to pray but to make conversation while she enjoyed breakfast from a tray – an appetising spread of toast triangles (white), crinkled pats of butter, a blob of marmalade and tea from a bone china pot. All this she downed, propped up against her pillows in a pink frilly nightdress and, in winter, a white crocheted bed jacket.

When she'd finished, dabbing her lips in regal manner, all children were shooed off to make their own breakfast in the school kitchen. The cook, small and fat and named Mrs Long, didn't begin work until well into the day. I was so small that if it was my turn to make breakfast, I had to drag up a chair to reach the grill. Regularly, I started small fires so whatever I and my friends dished up was invariably charred, as were we.

It was curious that Mip, who had already enjoyed breakfast, then sat at the head of the table and took delivery of a second rack of silver toast. Perhaps it was the same rack replenished – but by whom? If you were fortunate enough to sit next to her and able at such an early hour to muster sufficient charm, she might offer you a slice of her toast, which did indeed seem like silver when she swiped her knife across it.

I have related this story often to pupils when they are after an anecdote or a biscuit. I try to explain that this was standard boarding school practice in the late sixties of the twentieth century; that life then was *pretty weird, if you ask me*. I then urge pupils back into a consideration of the universal – surely the main point of teaching – with questions such as: 'What does it mean to be normal anyway?' Usually, they retort with: 'Anyone know what's for lunch?'

On Sundays, the pupils of Pippins went to church, an institution which had nothing much to do with God. Its message was rather about clothes: brown walking shoes, blue woollen dresses – in summer, gingham – blue coats, handkerchiefs and a walk.

The vicar of Axminster had no time for children, indeed seemed oblivious to the twenty-six little girls and a girl-boy in front of him. His lesson began each week with the unpromising words: 'And my text for today is…' by which point my mind was half way up old Firry, eating toast, at home by the fire, in the village shop purchasing a red exercise book…

More memorable was a particular walk to church that brought me back to earth – which is to say that it hurt. Yolanda was at the centre of it, shoving me against a hedge, then up on to a bank and shouting words to the effect that 'just because you wrote a story it doesn't mean you're special. You're not special. You're very boring and you smell.' It was the first time I had been met with such unbridled anger at close quarters, not to mention the personal insult. I was often told as a child that I smelt. Once, in the cinema, my ten-year-old sister announced that I stank. At secondary school, I was summoned by the housemistress to be told that I reeked.

'Where?'

'Everywhere. Your armpits smell, your mouth smells and in general you smell. And it's something you need to know.'

I am still proud of my stoicism. For I took very little notice and continued, with blocked sinuses, to walk around with my mouth open, running at top speed around the school, without a care for deodorant or toothpaste. Now I go nowhere without a toothpick.

The cause of Yolanda's fury was an incident a few nights earlier. At about ten in the evening, Mip had barged into the dormitory, walked straight up to my bed and demanded what was the matter.

'I can't get to sleep.'

'Why not?'

'I don't know.'

'Well try.'

'I have tried.'

'Well, why don't you write a story?'

'No paper.'

Within seconds Mip returned with an old exercise book and a biro.

I eagerly set about writing what was to be the second or third volume of my childhood oeuvre – an Enid Blyton-style narrative which was soon lovingly typed out by my brother's godmother. She wrote slushy novels – published to boot – and lived with a lady in Kensington who had a man's voice and a large pimple on her chin.

Worse than the bullying moment on the way to church was another that injured more, for the fault line, like a crack in a tooth, is still there.

Pippins was regimented. The breakfast routine was regimented, the number of sweets, home time, term time all regimented too. There was even a timetable dictating when you could visit the lavatory. Bowel opening was scheduled for the evening and there was only one lavatory. I can still feel the dirty warmth of the wooden seat on which, one evening, I perched in a desperate attempt to relieve myself of the filth of the previous week.

Push, push. Nothing.

A bang on the door.

Another bang.

A shout.

'Hurry up!'

More pushing.

Then the beginnings of something. But only the beginnings.

It was at this point that Mip, once more in frilly nightgown and pom-pommed slippers, dispersed the queue, opened the door, lifted me off the seat, pathetic cheroot in full view, and transported me to her own bathroom. I sat staring at a gauzy pink ball that looked a little like my cherished tutu, hanging off one of the bath taps. I believe I wept, if not out loud then certainly inside. I have struggled ever since with the business of the bathroom. I rarely cry, other than in the bathroom, where much of my reading is also done. As yesterday, when gov.uk sent an email, reference ZZ21D27182 with the opening statement: The decree absolute has been made and you are now divorced.

I had another encounter with a bathroom when at nine in the evening, again sleepless, I was passing the time of night with the girl in the bed beside me. Mip or Matron, one of whom had been lurking about, stood in the doorway and told us talkers off – once, twice. The third time, I was stopped mid-flow, instructed to get out of bed, no slippers or dressing gown, feet straight onto the cold floor and 'Follow me please, now, and by now, *I mean now!*'

Then came a ghastly command:

'Get in there!'

In there was the bath.

'Until I come back and fetch you.'

She didn't suggest that I recline in the bath, neck-deep in hot water scattered with rose petals or Himalayan salts, smoking one of my father's pipes. No. I was to lie in a cold, empty tomb, an act of cruelty for small living beings of any species.

A long time passed.

No Mip.

Nobody.

Hours.

Any memory of my salvation and return must have been frozen out by the chilly sensation of cast iron through pyjamas.

On occasion, night could spring the opposite experience. One of Mip's favoured marketing ploys was to hustle you out of bed to meet prospective parents. 'Please put on your winter dress and come downstairs.'

Winter dresses were a blue shift. The scratchy material was chosen by the school, but parents were allowed to style it as they pleased. Mine had been designed by seamstress and stand-in mother of what finally amounted to forty years – Sylvia Lewis (known as Lu-Lu).

Mip liked the dashing look Lu-Lu had come up with, and wished it to be paraded around her drawing room to impress a couple of Saudi Arabian visitors. A lot of clucking went on. In my excitement, I hadn't brushed my hair which had been chopped off a week before I became a boarder and had grown into an unattractive helmet to complement the chaos of my teeth. Notwithstanding, the Arabians were charmed. I was sent back to bed with a toffee – only to be woken by someone plopping into the communal chamber pot which sat in the middle of the room every night in order to stop anyone from leaving the dormitory.

On reflection, I feel these incidents must have occurred in the summer term. For, not long afterwards, my father arrived with a horse-box to take the school donkeys home to our farm. My sister had asked for this; and it must have been a relief to Mip, who wouldn't want to be hampered by children or donkeys in the holidays.

I lack much affinity with animals. I don't dislike them, but nor do I gravitate towards them in the enviable way of my sister. For a while, this made me feel morally inferior, so I wrote gushing fables about dogs and cats, in an attempt to feign interest, as well as to gain the attention of that godmother – she who wrote romantic novels and typed out my stories, and who, more importantly, would have me to stay in Kensington. Once she bought me a pink miniskirt from Carnaby Street with a belt punched with gold-rivets.

She and her lady friend were animal lovers, but in the right way. I was strangely charmed by the dismal yapping of their sausage dog because, never far away, was the purr of a printing press. Animals in their small house in Abingdon Road, were kept in proper proportion to the more important business of life. Whereas at Yarde, they were talked about too often, were far too much everywhere and all day. Later, when I was a nun, animals were considered an irrelevance. Indeed, anyone who ate too much was likened to a dog ('which remember is God spelt backwards, just as boy is yob').

The donkeys spent the summer in the orchard, along with other animals brought home from Pets's Corner. These included my rabbit, Zip, a quivering ball of hostility. Zip represented the worst in me, and finally ran away into the deep grass of the Lotus Pottery garden next door.

'THE LUNATICS'

(1)

Before you weigh in with objections, let me explain that lunatic was a term my father used to describe any relation, stranger or acquaintance of whom he was particularly fond, or – however they might be afflicted – he found entertaining.

I seem to have had a lot to do with people who fall under this, his category. The first was in toddlerhood when all three Church children were regularly chased around the village by a woman in black, who liked to jab her walking stick in our direction, pull up her skirts and yell threats at high volume. Most exciting was one Sunday in church when the congregation was singing 'Conquering Kings their Title Take', and I lay stretched beneath the family pew colouring in a butterfly's wing. Suddenly there was a bash to the heavy church door and the mysterious anonymous person fell into the porch. Restoring herself, she moved to the aisle and began conducting the hymn, using her walking stick as a baton. The congregation, enchanted by this interruption, stared and kept singing until finally she was ushered like royalty to a pew where she sat quietly until the offertory hymn.

My father was a churchwarden. While he disapproved of people describing out loud how God had intervened in their lives, or why it would be a good idea to attend or host an at-home prayer group or Alpha class, he took his religion seriously, never missing Matins and forcing himself to turn up at training sessions to which his role on the parish council committed him, along with the miniscule verger.

It was my father who first labelled the woman a lunatic, and he saw no hypocrisy in treating her at the same time with impeccable politeness. Head bowed and solemn, he carried the collection plate, arriving at her pew, and waiting as she rammed a hand down her stocking to fish out a few large pennies from her bulging ankle. My father, like one of Oscar Wilde's butlers, showed no emotion other than a pleasing gleam of irony, after which he resumed his journey down the aisle in step with his fellow churchwarden.

The nature of this, the first lunatic in our lives, was particularly pleasing. One night, who knows why, she rose from her bed and started walking in her pink winceyette nightdress to the bus stop where, at daybreak, she took a ride to Paignton. Somewhere along the way, she was ditched by the bus driver and picked up by the police, never to be seen again. Her sudden disappearance was the best end to a much-loved story re-told over and over throughout the first quarter of my childhood.

The next person of unsound mind was Bill, an employee at Pippins. His first job of the term was to carry school trunks from car to hall and up the front stairs to the appointed dormitory. His second, to lurk about the lavatories mopping the floor.

Bill was dear and harmless, while also being pleasantly frightening, for he had a habit of fixing his eye upon the nearest child or adult. Was he remunerated for his services? Probably not. For as soon as he'd carried a trunk upstairs, he would reappear and glare at my father who would pile up a few old pennies to hand him, before breaking into a breathless fit of giggles, a habit of boyish charm he sustained into old age.

At my third school, mental illness played a yet more riveting part. Here, the nastier side of the mid-twentieth century was doing its bit: it was a time when victims of insanity were locked away. And, in our case, the school chose to involve itself with an institution aptly called Coldharbour, perhaps in order to fulfil its charitable status.

The first foray into the world of Coldharbour demanded that small girls walk in pairs to a local hall where, unsupervised, they were to play games with some of its most troubled victims. Among their playmates was an unnerving person whose features had been so disarranged at birth that his eyes, nose and mouth seemed to have been chucked in the direction of his face, where they'd landed at random. This long pre-dated my life as a nun, when I was taught to think of all people not as bodies but souls, and thus to discount their appearance. I was terrified by the look of this four-foot Bilbo Baggins whose left eye was adjacent to his nose. More frightening still was a devastatingly handsome, six-foot blond of about thirty, who would have been an object of desire had he been seen singing madrigals in the Abbey.

For the entire encounter, whether galloping, skipping, walking hand in hand with a lunatic, the blond hunk followed me around at a slow pace, eyes boring into my back. I was able to take pleasure from the other bizarre characters in the room, but this man provoked only terror. He had a look of purpose on his face that was most unnerving, as if he was planning an assault. My recurrent dreams about him were no longer fabricated for effect. I must eventually have written home to complain, for a day came when we were released from the duty of visiting the hall. Worse, we took to visiting the hospital itself.

One year, the school performed *Hansel and Gretel* on Coldharbour's stage. Unable to hold a solo note for long, I had been assigned a small part in the chorus, which meant wearing a beige-coloured belted tunic and a pair of brown tights that sagged at the crotch. My housemistress, whose legs resembled those of a grand piano, taught us the songs after evening prayers, stabbing the air with her small hands, an irritable manner of conducting she carried into old age.

On the afternoon of the performance, the hall at Coldharbour was packed. The minute Hansel appeared on stage, and before (s)he had begun singing, frenzied clapping followed. Not far into the performance, a gaggle of inmates ran up onto the stage where they snatched cast members from the wings and waltzed them in their arms, with yelps of wild delight. This was the cue for someone to let out a scream, which in turn brought the old red velvet curtain crashing down. All lunatics were swiftly removed, while the cast, shaken and bewildered, was whisked back to school on a bus that smelt of old carpets.

Another lunatic, so-called for she didn't conform to any conventional routine or behaviour, was a relation of my father, known as Auntie Noo. She was said to have caught sleeping sickness in Africa, as a result of which she was only ever to be seen tucked up in bed, her slack, doughy head propped up on a pillow and just visible above the crisp oblong of her top sheet.

One year, when I was four or five, the family was with her on Christmas Eve. As we processed away from her bed through to the adjoining sitting room, I caught sight of a porcelain angel on her mantelpiece. My spirits soared, not because of what the angel signified – Christ or crypt – but because of the stocking that would appear at the end of my bed next morning. It was the only time in my life when early rising was a pleasure. Even so, it was the moment of anticipation in Aunty Noo's sitting room that I remember most vividly. Each Christmas was the same, whereas this moment was of itself and struck my soul as the closest I could get to experiencing bliss. This is why I now number myself among the lunatics who belong firmly to no place, time, person or belief. Instead, I float somewhere freely between.

Once, when my brother and I were staying with Aunty Noo on our own, we were taken by Sister Murphy, the Catholic nurse who looked after her, on foot through the hedge-lined lanes to a nearby church where the choirboys, dressed in red with white ruffles, jeered at us in our smart coats.

On the way back, one of us wanted a pee. We were cavalier about this. All our small lives we had 'been' behind bushes, trees, barns, sheds – anywhere we could find. However, Sister Murphy, who wore for a hat something that looked like a cup-cake holder, was disapproving.

But Aunty Noo.

Why did we so love her? Why not be cruel about her lying in bed all day? Our mother was disparaging about people who rose late. She made it her business to know the hour of rising of just about everybody in the village. Perhaps the fact that doctors were involved, or that Noo had acquired her affliction in Africa assuaged her? Whatever it was, something of Aunty Noo's spirit permeated her house, opening doors and freeing our spirits, which were in some odd way cramped and confined within the walls of Yarde.

After Auntie Noo, the other ritual for a proper Christmas, was to visit the family's graves in Dawlish – along with a cousin called Susan, and her parents Bet and Donald. Lunatic was not a word applicable to Donald, nicknamed Donnie. Worse, he was a nonentity because he was shaped like a small pillar box and spent his leisure hours sucking boiled sweets. He had also been in the army which, by father's reasoning, was a service inferior to the Navy, though tentative research reveals that he played an important part in a prisoner of war camp during the second world war. *Not a proper man* was my father's private opinion. Or not so private when at home, post-gin and for that precious hour before supper, when every man and his dog had their place in his nightly jeremiad.

Then, Donnie would simply be one among many 'bloody lunatics' or, if they were female (the Labour MP, Mrs Gwyneth Dunwoody, for example), 'bloody maniacs'.

Aunt Bet was more formidable. Made in the image of Mrs Long, the small round cook at Pippins, her tendency was to sit legs apart to reveal a flabby view of her stocking tops. Night and day, she wore a hair net and often slapped her thigh, exclaiming: 'How awful.' That meant she was feeling pretty good and was in full acrimonious swing.

Once in the graveyard, everyone set to on a spot of weeding, for all of my father's ancestors were laid to rest in that grand plot. Later, his cousin, Arthur Frederick Daubeney Olav Eveleigh-de-Moleyns (Lord Ventry), known as Cousin Bunny, a lunatic bachelor from Bournemouth who was mad about dirigibles, blimps, hot air balloons and cream cakes would join them. When our grandmother was ill after a stroke, Cousin Bunny went to visit her in Dawlish Hospital, brandishing a bunch of bananas. In her stroke-induced dementia, she mistook the bananas such that, on his arrival at her bedside, she threw back the blankets, lifted her nightdress and waved her legs in the air as if riding a bicycle. Bunny, a Catholic virgin (so far as we knew), was so shocked that he beat a hasty retreat. On his demise in 1987, Bunny was one of the few to be given a grave behind high gates, his existence celebrated by a swanky headstone with copperplate lettering. Such pomp was considered by his quick relations to be in bad taste, so his tomb was only ever given a cursory weeding.

The best part of the graveyard visit was lunch at a hotel, where the table at which they ate came to be merged in my mind with the one in the dining room at Pippins. The food was never as good as Yarde's, but redeemed by the fact that we were on an outing which required our father to be present, not just in body but in mind. As he lies merged now with the Devon soil above the River Dart, I can still hear his laughter, slightly louder than usual, as if it tired him to react generously on cue.

Pudding downed, we scooted back to the Wolseley and were driven home in a blur of car-sickness brought on by the food and the fumes from our father's pipe, as well as the dogs panting open-mouthed in the boot. The sickness evaporated as soon as one of us three children was instructed to open the big green gates and the car slithered across gravel into the refuge of Yarde, where all opinions and prejudices for or against lunacy could be expressed freely.

'Oh yes, her. Well, she has to take tablets for her nerves.'

'Well, he was dropped on his head at birth so you can't count him.'

'Of course, there are too many of them. I heard the other day that they have it off while the potatoes are boiling.'

'What do you expect? She's a potter!'

'Anyone with a Jack Russell must be mad.'

In fact, anyone with a personalised number plate, a vegetarian diet, a penchant for sequins, patent leather, nail varnish, Babycham, a fear of mud, a disliking for boats, a collection of motorbikes, going for a drive in the countryside and eating junk food inside the car, without braving the Sticks (perhaps they feared it was the Styx!); watching TV before lunch, calling themselves Colonel, sporting a moustache, sideburns, dyeing their hair, buying new furniture more than once every forty years, net curtains, holding their knife or fork as if clutching two pens… was dubbed a lunatic, more or less.

And yet how sane and lovely were those endless walks up and over the green fields between Brixham and Paignton, the summer sea to the left, the dogs bounding, the arrival at Elberry Cove, lying on the shingle, searching for seahorses, mussels, popping seaweed, scanning the horizon for ships, closing one's eyes against the sun until the pupils became black, horizontal ovals, that Devon air…

THE MATERIALIST

Yarde was bought in 1961. The reason for moving from Somerset is a mystery, unless it was to quell the grief at the loss of Andrew.

The bereaved couple went away on what was intended to be a restorative weekend, taking the dog with them. I would love to know now how they talked to each other. Perhaps their spaniel was the truth-speaker, for on a trek along cliffs she scarpered as I do, too fast, and straight over the edge and out of this world, rolling over and over until the sea, let us hope, washed her away – as gently as it took Simon in that beautiful passage from William Golding's novel *Lord of the Flies*.

Perhaps it was the impossibility of finding the right action to match one loss so fast upon another.

Perhaps the memories of dead comrades at Normandy, or the realisation that he was now too old to play drunken pranks with friends – uprooting statues from the village green and cramming their broken limbs into a red telephone box in the middle of Cossington…

Who knows?

But one day he took a car journey back to his birthplace in Devon. To return to his own beginnings…

The night before leaving, this religious man who

didn't believe in visions, messages, magic, saw in his dream a flight of pink stairs, at the top a curtain, behind it a bathroom.

He happened upon Yarde only to discover it was for sale. In he walked, on the off chance or accompanied by some pre-warned agent. And there before him were the stairs of his dream, there the curtain...

And in his possession, the money.

Nine thousand pounds.

Once settled in Yarde, we children were introduced to a painting of an Italian fruit seller that hung adjacent to the signalling pink curtain that concealed the bathroom door. 'He's called Pipi.' The face of the fruit seller was as comforting as milk. In a subconscious rehearsal for the nunnery, where I sat for hours staring at the picture of the community's founder with his deep eyes and shifting expressions, I perched for entire afternoons on the carpeted stair before Pipi.

Beneath the side table at the bottom of those pink stairs was a large copper bowl. On birthdays, the significant moment was not a materialist one. It was Pipi. Slowly, hand softly held, the birthday child would be led to the copper bowl, and inside would be a mountain of fresh fruit.

'It's from Pipi.'

The tradition was maintained for so long that I cannot remember a single present during my teens other than non-birthday gifts bought by my father from Harrods, which he visited on his mysterious missions to London for the Navy. These were the most exotic of gifts – underwear for my mother, huge boxes cushioned by satin containing lipsticks and perfumes, and peculiar items for the children: gold chain belts and once, for me, a turmeric-coloured top made of material like bubble wrap. I wore it to a party held in a castle that stood on an outcrop of rock marking the meeting of the River Dart with The English Channel after its forty-seven-mile journey from the Moors.

All possible boys ran from me as if the orange of my top were fire.

It was a childhood lurid with acrylic, polyester, polycotton, bri-nylon, plastic… My hair had a static look as if I had just ripped a woollen hat from my head; my arms and legs were dragged through yellows, limes, pinks; stick-thin shins peered out of home-sewn, multi-patterned, too-short flares. Small wonder that in pique or despair, at twenty, I shaved my head, turned into a boy and wore nothing but workers's dungarees, or occasional cheesecloth for lightness. Were life an idyll, I would have lived naked, taking the sun on the lawn – like my aunt who spent her middle years lying au naturel beneath Willows, in the faux-fresh air of North London's Totteridge. I have a favourite photo of myself at four, naked but for a watering can, cascading the largest flowerbed with water drawn from the rusty tap just outside Yarde's stable back door.

My earliest sensual delight came when the family had just moved and the carpet fitters were at work. I bumped along behind them, in awe at the violence as nails were banged into corners. The second they dashed out to their van for lunch, I shuffled towards a green-blue remnant and crammed it into my mouth. It was new to discover that mismatch between eyes and taste buds. As I spat out the ball of tweed, Coxwain, the family dog, made the same mistake. He dog-coughed a couple of times, then wandered out through the French windows to eat grass and be sick into an outcrop of groundsel.

Between the ages of three and eight, all three children were taken to Clarks in the dull seaside town, Paignton, where they were escorted to an area furnished with thrones to have their feet measured for length and width by a Brannock device which fitted around their toes and heels. There was something exotic about the dullness of the wait and the fact that they never knew what might emerge in the arms of the shop assistant as she appeared from her store cupboard behind a pile of green boxes.

The purchase made, frequently I would sit on my bedroom floor, before me the cupboard knocked up by my father in an outhouse, from where I would gaze at my shoes, sniff them, even stroke and lick them, as if without taste I was flying above my body.

The materialist incidents I am now most ashamed of involved theft.

I craved the sound of plinking coins. My father was a plinker. Everywhere he went, he plinked, just as everywhere he went, he puffed on an unlit pipe.

One bored Saturday, I trespassed upon the dark maroon-carpeted end of the house where there were three rooms we rarely visited as children: a spare room, our parents' bedroom and my father's musty dressing room. I chose the third, climbed onto a commode of broken wicker, slid my fingers across a heavy brown chest of drawers and snitched a pair of gold cufflinks that adorned a photograph of his mother in a cloche hat. All that morning, I walked around the garden plinking.

Sundays were the only day my father changed out of his aertex shirt into a full black suit and waistcoat purchased from Gieves. And with this change of costume came a change in manner.

'Where are they?'

'Where are what?'

'My cufflinks.'

A kerfuffle ensued as I remembered my offence. I was generally forgetful, preferring new impressions, smells, thoughts, words, as though the moment before had somehow never existed. The church service chugged on boringly as ever, but my father's head was in turmoil, until he accused me straight out: 'You've got them. You've got my cufflinks!' Was he apprised by God? 'And if you don't find them, we're not going to the beach. Not this afternoon. Not ever. I suggest you go and look for them.'

My mother took a trowel and yanked me towards the raspberry canes. I wanted to cry, for I knew the cufflinks might have dropped silently from my pocket into the soil while I had been playing. Suddenly it seemed a very big garden – a great graveyard where somewhere, deep or shallow, the dead gold lay.

Half way through the search I had an idea.

'I need a stick.'

'What do you mean, a stick?'
'Like the man on the beach.'
'What man?'
'The man with the stick.'

Once, on a trip to the beach, I had spotted a lone figure in an anorak walking head bowed, with a stick, at the end of it some kind of hook. Now and then, he raised the stick in the air and retrieved something from the end of it which he put in a bag that hung round his neck. When I had asked what he was doing, the phrase *metal detector* made no sense. But I decided that what the man on the beach had had was what I needed now.

I was left ferreting until lunchtime. Under the anaesthetic of sun, I lost energy for the search and was more interested in the sky. When called for lunch – the kind that punctuated the first twenty-one years of my life – I was sad to leave the garden.

'Any luck?'

Sideways nod.

The telephone rang halfway through a mouthful of bread sauce.

To reach the phone at Yarde, you had to walk from dining room to sitting room, an open plan area that had no feel of equivalent arrangements favoured today. Whoever it was that took the call bumped into the sofa on the way, shoving it on its castors so that it stood at an angle to the fireplace. And there they were – the cufflinks, gleaming on the inedible blue-green carpet, set at an angle to each other as if in conversation.

We went to the beach after all.

As for Christmas, that was never a festival whose meaning we were encouraged to consider. The business of articulated belief was regarded as vulgar. Life was metonymic and Christmas, a feast.

At six, I was given a doll by my grandmother together with a selection of hand-sewn clothes. The doll had long blonde hair, which I was quick to cut off, loving the swish of blades through nylon. Notwithstanding, this present was temporarily the answer to the question of who made the universe and why. It provided hours of entertainment, along with the other gift from my parents – a flimsy red case with white stitching containing Sellotape, a packet of biros, a notebook, paper clips and other cheap stationery items, the spaces between filled by scrunched pages of *The Daily Telegraph*. Nothing more was needed for happiness. Only peace and hours to myself in my bedroom, where I lay on my front, head close to the cupboard, beneath a cheap, green vanity washbasin. There I would scribble in a notebook, trying out new words, writing over and over in different coloured biros that had to be rolled between palms to encourage their flow.

One year, when I had grown out of dolls and was fixated once more upon shoes, my mother drove me to a budget shoe shop in Torquay and told me I could choose whatever I liked. This unusual announcement filled me with fear. I knew that these shoes were cheap: cream patent leather strap shoes with a bow, pointed green pumps with a small heel and at least two others which my mother dumped on the counter. And on Christmas morning, there they were, bursting out of my father's shooting sock which, when unworn in thickets on the outskirts of Totnes, was used as a stocking. I flung the oranges and nuts to the floor.

Then sorrow.

For I had kicked aside the severity of childhood, indeed a lesson of life itself: that the greatest beauty is divided into small beauties, and too much of any beauty is diminishing.

If it wasn't cufflinks or shoes, it was rings.

Weekly, I tore open comics in the hope that a jewel would be secreted between pages of migraine-inducing cartoons. If lucky, I would wander into the unlit corridor behind our dining room, close my eyes and drop the newly acquired ring in a spot close to glass-fronted cupboards full of old china. After five minutes, I would return to come upon it as if it had been bestowed by an invisible patron.

On occasion, I smuggled a friend from the council houses into the playroom and we spread out all the rings we had collected over the years and swapped them.

My insistence on rings became more insidious by the time I was ten, and the Kensington novelist who had typed out my trash from Pippins came to stay for a week.

It was a ritual to rifle through our guests's suitcases in the hope of a gift. There was nothing in the novelist's suitcase, but on the dressing table, a gold ring of minuscule size replicated itself in the mahogany swing mirror. It fitted her marriage finger though it was designed as a signet ring.

'I like that.'
'I like that ring.'

'That ring is very nice.'
'I saw that ring when I was walking past your room.'
'Where did you buy that ring?'
'Did someone give it to you?'
'It's nice when people give you things, isn't it.'
'It's very nice. I like it. I like it, that ring…'

Only cowardice stopped me from asking if I could have it.

On the day of her departure, the novelist snapped, 'Take it!' Instantly, it lost its allure – though not without having something astonishing to say to me some nine years later.

I look back now with guilt at my obsession with stuff. I knew nothing of refugees, those for whom clothing means not beauty but warmth. I'm not so sure that I have absorbed this lesson even now. But if you happen to say you like a piece of clothing in my cupboard, it's immediately yours, and I can never walk past a homeless person without asking what they need. I even conduct research into how to help, but again and again I come up against the same bullish assertions: 'Well, he was offered sheltered accommodation but he wouldn't accept it because he couldn't get his drug fix if he did.' Or: 'He was in the army; he's beyond rescue.' 'Oh she's got mental health issues so it's her problem not ours.' Baloney. It's not true. Those with no roots plumb the world more deeply than most housed people I know. I have talked to so many who understand the exact way of the weather, accept the possibility of angels, understand the points of the compass and how to find the most comfortable position in a shop doorway.

At thirteen, I sat on the bed of a big girl at boarding school and watched as hair, candyfloss light, was turned with one flick into a loose and exotic chignon. For the occasion of some crude social gathering unworthy of her Parisian roots, she had cut off the top of an old maxi dress, turned it into a circular skirt which she complemented with a wrap-around top in mole cashmere worn without underwear. Her breasts were the most beautiful I had ever seen – small, tanned, upright, the aureoles a mystical dark circle, nipples large. I looked down at my own mammary glands as they began to bud, and knew there would be no stopping their version of enthusiasm. On and on they would go until twenty years later, in a fit of pique, I scraped together sufficient funds to have half of myself removed by a Chinese surgeon. I have always preferred androgyny.

Such vanities I still dream of as sins to be criticised by nuns. Periodically, in the moments before waking, I am treated to a vicious telling off for my choice of a bright turquoise top rather than a white sack. Still, I am glad to have returned to my own pure self, that being who knows what she loves and had, as a child, such a passion for jumble sales, despite the unappealing sound of the term. I attended them all in Stoke Gabriel's village hall. If nothing caught my eye, I ransacked my mother's dressing-up box for cast-offs from my grandmother who, on a tight budget in a tall house on Elm Row, Hampstead, still knew how to dress like an empress.

The thing for rings went on.

In the nunnery in India, achievements were often marked by the gift of a trinket. And nunnery life was all about achievements: listing virtues, writing about virtues, lecturing about virtues, getting up early, earlier, earliest. And not just for a few days. For weeks, months, years. Those who could sustain such efforts might, if lucky, be rewarded with a gold ring to replace the crude silver version that was given to all newcomers and looked like something that lurked in the bottom of the gobstopper machine which stood on Paignton's esplanade, next to a telescope.

I longed for such a ring. Thought I deserved it. I had already been given a badge, but who cares for badges with their pins and clasps?

Finally, I took the matter into my own hands and asked. The answer surprised me: 'If we give you a gold ring, we'll have to give everyone a gold ring.' There seemed no logic here. But they caved in, summoning me a few days later to a room where the senior nuns gathered to discuss practical matters. There, the ring was presented in a most indifferent fashion. And lo, in the years that followed, gold rings seemed to be everywhere on everyone – particularly on VIPS who, in medieval style, were spoilt with trinkets in return for generous financial donations.

I became aware of worldly hierarchies only as a teenager, when my father's fury about trade unions, class divisions, and the misuse of yokels' vowels stoked a fire in my breast as livid as my clothes. Only after his death did I realise that this slim, tall boy-man had never really had a childhood of his own. As for youth, he had lived the bravest stretch on Normandy's Sword Beach. Yet he still revered, like so many veterans, the military outfit that had exposed him to such carnage.

Until the business of equality obsessed me, I was as greedy as the next Western child. The outside world was so far beyond the privileged cocoon of Stoke Gabriel, where all my parents' friends were Admiral This, Captain That, and an ex-Spitfire pilot who serviced the multiple clocks in Yarde so they would chime in unison on the hour.

Captain That was the most beautiful of men; he made me feel shy. When I was a thirty-year-old nun, his wife asked if I might sit with him in their garden. He was dying of cancer: 'Do you think I'm going to fall off my perch?' I answered with cold reassurance that there was life after death.

Now the fire of mourning for an entire generation of relatives has sent up in flames my attachment to things.

THE PATIENT

Redolent of another lunatic asylum, Westwing was the name of the school I was shipped off to after Pippins. It occupied an eighteenth-century Gloucestershire mansion with turrets and a run-down temple in its grounds, as well as two ha-has but not much laughter.

Westwing was run by Mrs Barker, a woman so terrifying that even my father avoided her, particularly when she required him to set off the fireworks on bonfire night. It pained me to see his large hands shake as he crouched in the field trying to light a match. And my mother's amusement at his failure offered no consolation, for at ten I needed to look up to him.

What occupied his mind in those public moments involving fire, when bonfires and the hearth was what he most loved at home?

Mrs Barker was another female with an interesting line in teeth (false), lower jaw not quite meeting the upper, so she seemed to be permanently masticating. She was also afflicted by an arthritic condition that meant she had to stick her arms out behind her to keep her balance. She was at least a hundred years old. A grown-up daughter used to visit for lunch in the vast school dining room that, once again, has become confused with another dining room, described by Michael Morpurgo in *The War of Jenkins' Ear*, one of the children's books I most enjoyed teaching during my long career in the classroom.

The pupils at Westwing slept in dormitories. These, as at Pippins, were named after flowers – perhaps to suggest that life in this fearsome mansion was fragrant and anodyne. In my first dormitory, there were two sets of bunk beds at one end of the room and a dressing table overlooking a field. At the other, a single bed was occupied by a large blonde girl called something like Amanda Stockington-Jones – just the type to captain an Olympic hockey team. As prefect in charge, her habit was to demand whoever took her fancy to perform a small task, such as fetch her hairbrush or fold up her clothes. I could never square the frustration and weariness of being hauled out of bed with the pleasure at having been chosen.

My appearance has changed dramatically over the years – ugly phases, better phases, a very few good phases. Westwing constituted a good phase. People liked brushing my hair, which had grown from a helmet into a pleasant shoulder-length bob. Also, I had an endearingly fragile look and long legs, though the teeth were an eyesore.

When not in bed, my means of survival was to establish a foothold in sickbay. This involved a complicated rigmarole, but it was enjoyable, thanks to my penchant for dramatics and the sweetness of the Matron. Once or twice, Matron took me to lunch in a restaurant that memory tells me was suspended in mid-air above the Severn Bridge, height once again bringing pleasure.

My first ruse, arising from a real ailment exaggerated for effect, was to complain of a sore throat. I would queue up outside Matron's surgery, a small room with a cupboard full of promising-looking packages, pills and potions. A throat sweet would be pressed into a small hot hand. If I turned up seven times, I could have my temperature taken, – a pleasure akin to sucking a lollipop but without the flavour.

Sickbay was a bedroom beside a large boudoir with a four-poster bed and velvet curtains in which Mrs Barker slept. Alone. Sometimes, small children were treated to soft-boiled eggs and soldiers there, making it a satisfactory refuge of cosiness and mystery.

The only person of interest at Westwing was Mr Brown. Joseph Beuys, the artist lunatic who claimed he was rescued by Tartar tribesmen during the Second World War, said that in places like universities where everyone pretends to talk rationally, it is rare for an enchanter to appear.

Mr Brown was proof of Beuys's philosophy, which I later espoused as a nun: I learnt that it's not appearance that determines one's interest in a person, but the quality of their power. Like Mrs Barker, Mr Brown seemed ancient, wore a black gown and looked like a bird of prey, his nose hooked and huge, hair white and lips sucked-in, hair-grip-thin. But these factors were incidental. He was characterised by a curt strictness and, by some miracle of wit and clarity, he managed to make mathematics erotic.

Mr Brown would set tests that stood out for their seriousness. Would instruct the class to be silent or 'you'll know about it', while he read out questions at a pleasantly slow pace punctuated by a cough. One day he beckoned me to his desk, whose surface had the same ridged texture as the stew I had hated at primary school. The way he waggled his forefinger indicated that I was to approach silently. Standing beside him, heart pounding, one leg wrapped around the other, I waited as he folded his newspaper, took my exercise book from the bottom of a pile and opened it slowly. Without a word, he pointed to a mark written on the top right-hand corner: 99%. 1st=. I was peeved by the equals sign but, from that moment, I loved maths simply because I loved Mr Brown.

Any desire for achievement, however, would always be tempered by a hankering for toast. So I would, by means of a variety of manipulations, revert to sickbay. On occasions, the delicacy might arrive, accompanied by a soft-boiled egg. But the sport risked serious punishments. On one anxious trip to the bathroom, I was thwarted by the ghastly apparition of a toothless Mrs Barker, white hair waist length, like one of *Macbeth*'s weird women. At the sight of me, Mrs Barker made a growling sound and slammed the door, taking time to run a bath while I waited outside.

Real illness forces maturity upon you, shoving you hard up against your body and putting an end to pretence. I knew a smidgeon of such maturing when I was transferred from Matron's nest to a hospital in Temple Meads, Bristol. All I can see now is a square room, six beds counterpaned in green, two strangers sitting up behind trays, and a bed near the window where I spent a week recovering from a tonsillectomy.

I remembered little about being gassed into sleep in a dentist's chair a year earlier, other than a dream of a gnome flying upside down into a hole. But I felt cheated at remembering nothing about being eased into unconsciousness for the tonsillectomy. I was particularly disappointed at not having seen what they called the recovery room, an alliterative phrase that appealed to my sense of order.

Once back in the ward, I struggled not to vomit, before giving in and shrieking at a nurse to bring the kidney-shaped bowl that was made of the same rough card as the trays used at home for chickens's eggs. I have always been afraid of vomiting. I had an aunt who spent much of her early middle-age in a state of mild nausea. She recounted with some pride that when pregnant and expected to escort her husband to functions, she mastered the art of vomiting into the nearest vase of flowers without anyone noticing.

In hospital, my throat was sorer than it had ever been. But, with an imperiousness forgivable only in a child, I asked the doctor if he would show me the operating theatre. It remains a mystery why he thought such special treatment was deserved, for I was after all neither the child of a celebrity nor the victim of poverty. But I was duly rigged up in a blue and white spotted gown, my paltry weight flicked onto a trolley, wheeled into a lift, and taken into the theatre where they showed me a real needle of sleep, and the white wellington boots that the surgeon had worn while operating.

Back to school for an entire term of nothing. But doing

nothing is underrated in schools. Early on in that unfresh beginning, I spent a weekend with a girl I didn't know well but liked; dark hair, pebble-thick glasses and troubled in some way. Her house was somewhere near Mr Brown's, which disappointingly snuggled at the top or bottom of a cul-de-sac, a term my parents could only use in disparaging tones. On the first morning, seated at a kitchen table in a house that had something of the same quality as my friend's spectacles, I ate a large bowl of well-sugared cornflakes.

But, as usual, it was the journey not the stay that mattered. I sat among school pals in the back of the car. Beside the driver, in a most mysterious manifestation, was Mr Brown, whose own car had perhaps broken down, unless he always went home with this family? Besides the realisation that he had a life outside the classroom and not in his academic gown, there was his head. I stared at the back of it, noted its slightly triangular shape, the thinning of his hair which poked over his macintosh collar, and I knew that Mr Brown was unhappy. This 'fact' in turn made me miserable in the without-warning-sweeping-down-into-a-dark-place way that I have so often suffered when I see that a person I have loved is not, after all, the god that I thought they were.

Soon after Mr Brown fell off his pedestal, another ailment was manifested. Intuition instructed me that, without tonsils, I couldn't this time moan about my throat.

Thus, I transferred my attention to my stomach.

'It hurts.'

'Well come here so I can feel it. No, you're fine. Go to

bed.'

The following day, the same complaint.

'Right. Well, stand aside.'

Matron was a great deal less pleasant when not suspended over the River Severn in a restaurant; indeed, she was capable of quite a nasty measure of firmness. However, I soon magicked my way back into the warm womb that was sickbay.

When the feared but anonymous doctor arrived, Matron was standing to attention at the end of the bed as he announced: 'I'm going to insert this little thing up your behind; that should do the trick.'

My behind was categorically not a place to be fiddled with by a stranger. But at Yarde we had been taught not to fuss, a dangerously passive philosophy with which to saddle a child. Thus, I duly presented myself and was then ushered to a lavatory with walls that stopped short of the ceiling. The explosion that followed was unsatisfactory because an explosion was all it was.

Once back in sickbay, I assumed the feebleness I now associate with Linton Heathcliff, that ninny of a character in *Wuthering Heights* whom Emily Brontë herself clearly intends us to despise. I duly informed Matron that I felt worse but pleaded with her not to fetch the doctor again as he should go to prison.

'Then you'll have to get better.'

Here was a dilemma. But soon, as always favouring drama over routine, I opted for the doctor, only to be rewarded by the obscenest experience of my young life: not a suppository but his finger.

Up my backside.

Followed by the announcement: 'You've got

appendicitis.'

Within an hour, sickbay was alive with the epileptic blue lights of an ambulance sweeping up the school drive and suddenly I was on a stretcher being carried straight back to another department of the same hospital from which I had been collected only months before.

Once again, as with all places featuring not beautiful trees but oblongs of rest, I can picture the ward as clearly as the typing fingers that now describe it: eight on each side, the door to the left, a bare wall to the right in a large square room with high windows. Next to me in a cot, a small boy with mottled skin staggers around on bow legs while, very soon, green curtains rattle around the bed and I am back in the bosom of anonymity.

'Put your bottom on the pillow.'

'No! Not again!'

'I'm afraid it's necessary in order to find out what's wrong.'

At this, I screamed, an unfamiliar doctor tutted and soothed but finally had his way, performing the examination of which grown men are terrified. When he had resumed a standing position, he removed his latex gloves and announced to the nurse next to him that the appendix was inflamed, a diagnosis which seems to me now to have been conjured merely out of misery.

Back in the ward after the operation, I adopted once more the Linton Heathcliff approach, whining and puling. My mother arrived in a hat made of acrylic petals, carrying a tin of coloured pencils, a new nightdress and some paper. Having trained before the war as a nurse and served in Oxford at the very college where I studied English eight years after the appendix fiasco, she proceeded to interrogate everyone on topics related to hygiene. This made me feel as violently on edge as when my father was unable to make a firework go off under the watchful stare of Mrs Barker.

One Sunday during my stay in the children's ward a Titan with a back-combed bun walked in carrying a disturbingly modern-looking bible. She sat on a chair in the middle of the room.

'Please sit up. It is the Lord's Day.'

I had been subjected to church all my life, and praying in bed seemed infinitely preferable to my father's chilly pew in Stoke Gabriel. However, in our home church, by virtue of their very presence, my parents had maintained order. Here, with the excuse of sickness and in the presence of a stranger, the infant patients wreaked as much havoc as it is possible to create given the restraints of high, hard beds. In those days everyone knew The Lord's Prayer, so I was untroubled when the Titan with doughnut bun, blue dress and bossy belt announced that we were to join her in: 'Our Father, hallowed dee dee dee, dee-dee-dee-dee thy-will be done...' I liked the word 'hallowed', for it seemed in some way to be connected with the tree I had climbed at Pippins. But it triggered the bow-legged boy in the cot beside me to begin a running commentary of his own making. This set up a wave of giggling from bed to bed until the whole ward was shaking. The Titan in blue simply soldiered on, like a troubled school-teacher without a lesson plan.

And so another term was spent at home eating toast, sleeping for whole days and nights at a stretch, and being commented on at frequent intervals as if I were something cooking: 'Still looks a little pale. Looks a little better. Soon be ready.'

But I wasn't ready. I hadn't yet returned to myself. Not until a term later. My last at Westwing.

One day, my maths lesson with Mr Brown was interrupted when the deputy head, also the French teacher, a Miss Clemes with buck teeth and no authority, walked in and commanded me to go straightaway to Mrs Barker's office. This wasn't an office but an old, dark sitting room with an open fire and two sprawled cocker spaniels.

There was a small, ridged desk in the middle of the room.

'There. Now sit and do the paper that's there.'

The paper that was 'there' was a maths exam and the first in a series of Common Entrance tests. No explanation. No preparation, no costly cramming. When I looked at the first question, I burst into tears because there was nothing much common about it. Mrs Barker butted her head in my direction, then suggested that if I wrote nought for the first question, I'd be on the right lines.

'But what about the second question?'

'Well, write something else for that. And stop crying. Look you've made a mess of the paper. Now we'll have to start again. I'm going to sit here and you're going to write down whatever I tell you to write!'

Thus, we made our way through the maths paper. I thought the ordeal was over, but Mrs Barker said, 'You'll have to come back tomorrow to write two other exam papers.'

'But I don't know anything.'

'Well, read this. This page.'

And she handed me a bible, her nasty lumpy finger pointing to a passage about Moses. That night, on the bottom bunk in Bluebell dormitory, I read about the burning bush and the tablets.

'Right, now you're going to sit the religious studies paper.'

When the question invited an outpouring about Moses I relaxed, just as I did when the English paper asked me to describe a day in the life of a pencil – I enjoyed a task that involved no facts.

But then, history. I had no idea about history, and still have rather a shaky sense of England, Europe, the world as it was in the past, feeling that I must have been residing in some other dimension when the Romans were forging straight lines across England. Mrs Barker saw my distress, and we navigated the difficulty together thus: she would retrieve a book from a shelf above her sofa, read out the relevant extract, and I would write it down in my own words. Not as easy as it sounds.

A few days later, we girls were waiting outside the locked cupboard in which our tuck was stored, when Matron came pelting down the corridor in her blue uniform. Rattling along behind her was a giant crimson sausage on a trolley. It was Mrs Barker, usually so fierce and formidable, now laid so low that everyone burst into tears. For she was being rushed to hospital. She had, we were told, been violently sick then suffered a heart attack.

She was never seen again.

THE NON-ACADEMIC

My father used the term 'Common Entrance' only to describe a work-person's means of entering a building. But one month after the event, my parents were informed by Sherborne that, conditional upon term-time performance, I was to be awarded a scholarship.

My mother started up all her elaborate networking activities. By now, either lonely herself or wanting the best for her youngest child, she thought it a good idea to contact the mother of every prospective Sherbonite who lived within a radius of twenty miles and invite them over for tea. Thus, I was introduced to a certain Mary Pryer, a Louise Brown and an Anna Someone with fine blonde hair. All three arrived in shorts and aertex shirts, along with their mothers. My mother pressed questions (or instructions?) on topics from clothes lists, trunks, guidance on the best way to reach Sherborne, whether by this A road or that...

Fees were never mentioned, money being a topic that ranked alongside sex, death and God. It is still a mystery to me whether my family was wealthy, posh-poor or how the fees were paid, given that my father was not enamoured of much in the way of work, other than strangling chickens and whacking pigs on the backside with a large white lollipop stick. Sadly, I was of little financial aid for, three weeks into my first term, I was found to be lacking in all academic ability and thus the glittering promise of a scholarship was withdrawn.

Though the word *thick* was never used, it was implied by teachers, elderly, dull and uninterested in children. Many had unappealing distinguishing features: one with brown skin tags hanging off her neck; another a wooden leg; a third, a voice that seemed wrenched from somewhere close by her ankles to make the sound of a Dalek with a toothache; the headmistress, who had a beautiful face and legs like sticks, was a victim of polio and looked like a seagull.

By the end of that term, I was moved from the top to the bottom sets in all but English. However, even English, later the only subject I cared for, was so dull that I can remember little of it, apart from the fact that it was administered from somewhere beneath the crash-helmet haircut of a person called Miss Austin who commanded her pupils – tender thirteen-year-olds – to write a sonnet.

Science was the greatest unknown. The Misses Burchardt taught biology. They were a pair of spinster sisters who lived on a farm in a neighbouring village; their goats defecated on exercise books and the only topic on the syllabus, as homemade as their jam, was flowers. Thus, for the length of each lesson, their pupils drew flowers, labelled flowers, cut off stamens, pinpricked anthers and pressed them, before gratefully forgetting them and, with books tumbling out of brown plastic totes, dragged themselves off to some other torture chamber of unlearning.

Physics was another mystery. And still is. An explanation would have been a good place to start, as in: 'I imagine this is your first physics lesson and, just in case you don't know, you shouldn't feel ashamed that you don't because you've never studied it before so, in a nutshell physics is x.'

No. Instead, we were told to pick up the toy Mini Minors from the bench before us and 'Measure them, chop-chop!' How one was to go about taking measurements was not something this teacher, a severe-looking person, posthumously famed for her contribution to the world of women's education, cared to explain.

She went on: 'Now, everyone up and follow me. We're going outside where there is a real Mini Minor and you are going to measure that.' Whose Mini this was or how the entire class managed to measure it, and with what, I have forgotten. But that's what we did, and afterwards returned to the laboratory which smelt of Jeyes cleaning fluid and gas. There we were told to calculate the relationship between the toy car and the real one. I have always cared about my relationship with reality, but this baffling instruction constituted the beginning and end of my relationship with physics.

Chemistry – no recollection. Only that it made me unhappy and that I gave it up after a couple of years, along with physics, history and geography. Geography has been reduced to a single fact. Not even a fact, a question: Where do oranges and lemons grow? Two marks.

We had a succession of maths teachers, the last being Miss Bell – a cross between a loaf of white bread and a Portobello mushroom. Unlike Mr Brown, she had no grip on the subject nor on the beings to whom she was imparting its mysteries.

Outside the classroom, I made friends fast, adding to Mary Pryer and Louise Brown a troupe of high-spirited thirteen-year-olds to play with. Leisure hours were spent running around the sports field, eating round upon round of white toast, smeared with margarine and jam, playing lacrosse and, when not seeking out the fuggish warmth of local hotels to partake of a thimble of sherry, going for walks on Plum Pudding. This was an old mound on the edge of the town where later we went to look for boys.

Life at Sherborne falls into two parts: the junior years, during which I careered around with blithe disregard for academic work; then the sixth form, when there sprung from nowhere a passion for study. The only teacher to support my efforts was Mrs Gill, a small dark-haired woman who taught French. A word of praise from this diminutive Scot was enough to transform a day and if, in her equally minuscule handwriting, she wrote 'good' at the bottom of a page of work, there followed a rush of real happiness. But I was deeply hurt when, after I had been made form captain, Mrs Gill commented in her report that I was good at looking after myself but showed no interest in the welfare of others. But it has always been true that I feel it none of my business to try and tell other people how to run their affairs. I would never dream, for example, of posting an instructional meme on a social media platform, even if it did issue from the lips of that most benign of teachers, Lao Tzu. And when I was a nun, I was no good at proselytising or suggesting that anyone should share my beliefs. I am still uninterested in telling people what not to eat, how to keep fit or how they should spend their weekends.

After Mrs Gill's candid report, I was turfed out of her French group without warning and transferred to one taught by a Mr Lewis from Wales. He was a very stupid man indeed; one of those teachers who comes into school with a blob of shaving foam on his chin and then yells so nastily you can't think straight.

As at Pippins and Westwing, all pupils slept in dormitories. These were even more severe than in the previous two schools: a long corridor divided into cubicles with a sixth-former at one end. There was no beauty in this arrangement, and I was unable to make my cubicle look anything other than clinical which, presumably, was the point.

Nights at Sherborne were dull. I managed to cajole a small apple-cheeked friend of great sweetness to stand on her bed in her baby-doll pyjamas, lean over our cubicle wall and read to me while I tried to get to sleep. Getting other people to do things continues to be a speciality. I have refined the art, pretty transparently, prefacing requests with a gushing compliment: 'You're so good at this… Would you mind…?'

Delegation has always come easily; navigation, on the other hand, is a mystery. My father thought this funny, but I have cried many a time when driving; ending up in Brighton instead of Devon, in a field instead of a house. I smashed a satnav once because the disembodied voice was so misleading in its use of the word 'recalculating'. And, when driving to meet an old lover at three in the morning, the same satnav, revengeful perhaps, grew so agitated that it might have been interpreted as a mystical message instructing that a swift return home would be best.

In the summer holidays that followed my first year at Sherborne, we had a family of Dutch cousins to stay. Whenever people visited from afar, a picnic was arranged and, on this occasion, my father pronounced: 'You go with Nel and Hank and then you can navigate.'

His smile. No wonder my mother fell for him.

The destination was only about three miles away, though even now I am unable to picture it, which was, of course, part of the problem. Wherever it was, the family had been there many times before, though when one has geographical shortcomings, the destination is of no consequence however many times 'before' one has been there.

So, out of the gate and turn right. Down the hill, past the pottery. Reach the war memorial; encounter a fork.

'Left!'

On… On…

'Straight, straight, straight!'

But at the end of straight, we seemed already to be in the wrong place. And that is the difficulty: as soon as you're in the wrong place, you keep being in the wrong place and the wrong place becomes more and more wrong. This is true of my life as a nun and now as an ex-nun, for I still live under the illusion that in all things there is only one correct route.

And suddenly we are in Paignton.

How we finally arrived is a mystery. Just as it is a mystery to me how I shall extricate myself from the fall-out of an unhappy marriage and forge another life somewhere in the great unknown of the outside world.

Perhaps, this time, my father didn't even say where we were going? Perhaps he had let the guests in on the secret and they were playing along with his ruse. At any rate, when we arrived, we immediately collapsed into the long grass of a meadow.

May there be a meadow to lie in here, now, soon, fifty years on…

At such moments of humiliation, I looked to an alternative father, Major J, who lived in the square Georgian house on the opposite side of the road from Yarde. Major J and his wife had recently retired from running a prep school. They were interested in our lives, in the explicit way our parents weren't.

Mrs J liked me less than her husband did. She thought me spoilt and thus behaved in a rather chilly manner towards my eagerness. Mrs J had very neat hair and looked classy in a headscarf, Queen Elizabeth-style, much as my mother and Brown Owl did. But she was a notch more sophisticated than my mother, certainly leagues ahead of Brown Owl in whom, by the age of thirteen, I had haughtily lost interest.

Mrs J was astute enough to recognise that my sister Jo-jo, as we called her, was a girl of sound character. Because Jo-jo cleaned out her rabbit. And, if she was cross, she showed it, whereas I was all for putting on an act, invariably involving the dressing-up trunk and cavorting about on the lawn, expecting to be watched and admired. Or, as when I started wearing a set of plastic buck teeth from Woolworths, laughed at. Perhaps it was simply a sign of my self-absorption that I thought Mrs J disliked me. The feeling may have issued not from Mrs J at all but from that troubling little faculty that was growing faster than my body – the conscience – telling me that there was something loathsome that instructed against exhibitionism.

Major J was the opposite of his wife. He loved me and I loved him. Everything about him: the way he smoked, his big floppy mouth and thinning white hair combed into vivid streaks across his white-spotted scalp; his handwriting, which was as beautiful as I thought a teacher's should be; the fact that he wrote me letters while I was at boarding school; and, most importantly, that at the end of each term, as soon as my report arrived in the post, he was there to treat me to a glass of Coca-Cola. For this reward, I would shoot up the hill, across the road and stand ready outside his large front door.

And the more my dunce-fulness had been pointed out by euphemistic criticisms, the more likely I was to receive his sparkling panacea.

The other treat Major J offered was a regular boat ride down, up or along the River Dart. In the summer, these were twice-weekly. And they were much better than the tedious aeons spent sailing our own dinghy which, in the name of fairness, was called Tianjo – an amalgam of our three names. When Major J took us out on his boat, all rigours and terrors of academic life, indeed life itself, melted away. There were no ropes to be yanked. If I steered, he offered me his captain's hat to wear then stood behind me, ensuring I did a good job, by doing it himself. At the heart of good teaching is not just expertise, but love.

A sense of order and contentment permeated both his boat, which was neat and clean, and the Scotch eggs which Mrs J made by hand. These were eaten at the point where the River Dart met the English Channel but, for all my geography, it might just as well have been the Atlantic or the Pacific. Sea is sea, after all.

Sometimes, when the sea was rough, my mother and I, two evaders together, would be despatched onto Torquay pier to make our way home on the bus. But if we were able, we endured the grey lollop of the waves and the gentle chug back up the River Dart in the dark, the twinkling lights of nearby boats as entrancing as Auntie Noo's Christmas angel. All the way, Major J would cough and splutter and light up his fags, and my father would sit in red canvassy trousers, legs twice-crossed, staring out at the water, at nothing, only breaking into laughter if required to be amused.

When the Js left Stoke Gabriel to live in Spain the Church family was bereft. Settled afar, if they ever did truly settle, they frequently invited our parents to stay. But my father resisted, as he did all trips that meant rising from his chair. They managed it once, for there is a photo of his long white body standing up in a swimming pool beside his wife in a bathing hat that looked like the chrysanthemums she tended in Yarde's flowerbed. Flowers still there today and, as this is being written, in bloom.

Now and then, the Js returned from Spain to stay. But it was never the same. Criticism permeated Yarde, and even I thought it odd that Major J took to bed half a cup of black coffee and smoked in the night. Nowadays, there is no limit to the oddity of my own night-time activities – drinking black coffee, white coffee, tea, hot milk, water, rice milk... But I draw the line at smoking, day or night, unless at a wedding. For weddings, unlike the joy of funerals, are invariably upsetting.

My last memory of Major J is a sad one. Mrs J had died from a stomach problem and he was staying at Yarde, so badly alone that it hurt to watch.

I must have been working as a writer's assistant in Topsham at the time. It was at the beginning of that peculiar phase which led me finally, like the disobedient daughter of some Shakespearean autocrat, to the nunnery.

One morning, Major J and I were walking together down the road past the Lotus Pottery where I had worked for a summer, past the Gabriel Court hotel where I had worked for another summer, past the war memorial to the post office where weekly I had bought exercise books as a child. Side by side, we were synchronised in sadness, he, agonising, and me in a different but equally profound mood of melancholy. What a fine moment it would have been to sit down beside the beloved River Dart and confide in each other. But we were each locked in reserve; each feeling that the other wouldn't understand. For at twenty-one I had never been bereaved. And at sixty-six, Major J had never considered becoming a nun.

As children, we rarely went on holidays. We live by the sea. What more do you want? Or were we even asked that question? Probably not, for we knew never to ask, which was why the first of only two childhood holidays was such a surprise.

'We're going to Scotland.'

I was seven or so then and excited into volubility. For, after hours, days, weeks, months, my father was at last prised out of his chair. We were used to my mother's diligence, after all. She was a heroic organiser of outings: beaches, castles, ruins, mansions; took us on walks to learn the names of trees; even arranged the occasional trip to the theatre. But our father? Never. Thus, whatever the cost to himself, his presence was a joy.

Assuming the role of Mr Brown, husband and father, for a fortnight he drove us in the old Wolseley up the A38, the A303 into Wiltshire, Hampshire, up, up, maybe even along the beautiful A262, his children dozing and arguing by turn, until at last we reached Yorkshire and a place whose name comes to me now as the Somerset village of Castle Cary, but couldn't have been. We were hundreds of miles away and, besides, the location was of no importance. It was rather the fact of our being together and staying in a down-at-heel hotel where we were assigned our own dining room. It was as if mixing with others would in some way lower us, although there seemed to be no others about and it might just be that it wasn't a hotel at all but just another rural manor owned by a female cousin with a man's name.

By the time we reached Scotland, all that remains is the sound of rushing river and the dining room table where we sat. I was in the same turquoise polo neck jumper I had worn for close on five years, and the hand-me-down orange shorts and shirt to match. What did we do? If my mother had had anything to do with it, we would have been sweating round places of historical interest. If my father was in charge, we would be sitting in armchairs reading, or, the rarest of treats, playing cards.

What of my mother's emotional state? Did she enjoy that holiday? Were she and her husband intimate? It didn't feel like that to us children, who had no idea of what intimacy was, other than the sharing of food and a car. But it is a happy memory. And Malta too, our only other childhood holiday away from Yarde.

This time the destination was St Paul's Bay where we rented a flat one Easter when it was warm enough to swim: my brother and I climbing over rocks, he in woollen red swimming trunks and me in a blue and white bathing costume. My father caught it on his clapped-out cine-camera, which he brought out every few months, after supper, so that we could watch it smoke and stall before black and white images shimmied into shape on a screen that rolled down into what looked like one of the gun cases he kept in his darkened study, amid pictures of dismembered animals and a large glass-covered bookcase containing sets of novels (abridged) in faux-leather, courtesy of The Reader's Digest. It was a film that was brought out at the reception to my wedding which featured childhood snippets and a decisive THE END at the point when, at twenty-two, I went, as far as my family were concerned, askew and turned into a Hindu.

In the second week of our Maltese holiday, when the beach with its large pebbles had lost something of its charm, we enjoyed a visit to Medina. Here was a town full of tall faded pink buildings that chimed with my sense of what was beautiful. When it came to matters of taste, I've always felt closer to Europe than to England. Not that I knew quite where Europe was, or where Malta itself was, let alone its history or geography.

In Medina there was an elderly cousin with a Marge Simpson beehive bun who, as usual, went by a man's name. She received the family for the afternoon, serving tea from a silver pot. After that, we took a speedboat to Gozo where there was another cousin – exotic – perhaps even an alcoholic, with a name I envied for it sounded French.

These two holidays were the jewels in our childhood because our father was there – involved, laughing, cracking more of his peculiar jokes than usual. Not joke-jokes with punchlines. He looked down on those, as he did on shop-bought cakes, though he ate enough of them.

How pleased he must have been, all the same, to arrive home to routine: my mother doing the washing on a Monday, hanging it out on a line that circled the vegetable garden, as well as the paved area where my brother and I played on a swing, pushing each other back and forth so hard that one day I went flying over the washing line and into a rose bush; where, too, while my mother pegged out the washing, he told me his first dirty joke:

'Right, listen to this. Why was the man breathing deeply?'

'How should I know?'

'Because he was coming.'

'Where from?'

Gales of laughter; me in tears.

THE ADOLESCENT

As we entered our teens, all energy was concentrated on finding local lovers. In my case, the hankering was for a young Mr Brown who might carry, and so help me evade, the weight of my ever-intensifying thoughts.

The secret search was conducted by corralling local friends and friends of friends into attics and basements where loud music would be played to which we danced wildly and with no style. As with all efforts in my life, these fell into a pattern, the repetition of which made them both successful and not, for it was God I was after, not a boy.

The evening would begin at the house of one of my two closest school friends, Mary Pryer, who lived in Newton Abbot. In Mary's bedroom, from where we could look out on the town below, we would don crimson bell-bottoms, a heavy coating of mascara and a smear of kohl pencil. This was surely sufficient to make us desirable.

After the ritual of dressing up, we would eat baked beans on toast and a fried egg, cooked by Mrs Pryer, a frightening person with pebble-thick specs and hair that could only be moved by a vast gust of wind. Then it was all about having ourselves driven by Doctor Pryer to somebody's house, once even down the steps into

Mary Pryer's own cellar with 'Rock Me For Christmas', or some other on-trend song blaring out of her brother's music system. I had complicated feelings for him. One day, when staying in the Pryer's holiday cottage in Trebetherick, we were rowing along the river Cam and I found myself besotted; the next moment, I wanted to run for my life and never see him again. However, his friend, Steve Someone from Teignmouth, was one of the few boys I wholeheartedly liked. He went to a school even posher than mine, and had a gentle face, which at one party he positioned close to mine, perhaps in the hope of a kiss? I shied away, as I have shied away from all things in life I have both wanted and feared – particularly kisses, which seem to carry all manner of dangers.

Steve Someone even came to Yarde. I squeezed myself once more into bell-bottoms and walked him around the village. It was at the half-way mark that we stopped outside The Castle Pub, one of the many village businesses where I later worked a season, serving fish and chips. There, he took off his shoe and I mine, as if this might preface a more manageable form of love-making. It was as far as we got, for though the need burned, touch was to do with the earth. And, for reasons still unknown, earth was the very place I was most keen to avoid.

Apart from Steve and Mike Pryer, there were no interesting boys in Devon other than a shepherd I fell for one evening in passing. Those we consorted with were as lacking in subtlety as were the clothes, the food and rural life in general in the early seventies. The whole rigmarole of getting dolled up as the preamble to courtship seemed pointless; it was the party itself that mattered. Though looking back, perhaps I have that the wrong way round.

Mary Pryer fared better, though she was to die at a tragically young age. The most interesting boys found her attractive. As we lay side by side in our sleeping bags at the end of such evenings, she regaled Loo and me with accounts of her conquests, for she was in many ways boyish in her designs and the first to know the meaning of that mysterious term: blow job.

The morning after each of these parties, we would rise late for another plate of baked beans and egg, rustled up by the noble and immobile Mrs Pryer. Then I would ring my father, who would rouse himself to motor along the A381 in his small van to collect me. We would return in silence, the dogs in the back, he puffing away on his pipe. Then it was back to Square One. No boyfriend and an endless wait for the next party. On it went, ad infinitum, for four long years.

Yet how optimistic we were; how we forgot about futility and hopelessness as news of each party was relayed by landline, and we would spend a day or so in preparation, hoping that the magical god-boy who knew how to think as well as to kiss, would pop out of nowhere and shine like the sun. And how suitable for an evader that none did.

There was one other boy I liked – a friend of my brother's called Pip, whose mother had died of cancer when he was very young. Pip had white-blond hair, was as pretty as my brother, and walked about all year round in a camel-coloured duffel coat. He was considered the best-looking of the local boys, but he was uninterested in me. Or indeed, in anybody and he was never heard to speak a full sentence. 'Better at woodwork' was how my mother explained him.

Years later, when I was at Oxford and close to my time in the nunnery, he turned up at Yarde with a girlfriend. At some point during the evening, while a party of sorts was going on downstairs, she and I went upstairs to my sister's bedroom, which I had hijacked as I did every bedroom in the house, apart from my brother's and my parents', for I was always in search of new atmospheres. We sat on the floor and looked at each other. It was very sudden the way the air changed as we began talking urgently. For at last, after all the years of feeling that my family was both very close and yet also distant, here was someone whose soul seemed my fellow. The unnamed girl must surely have felt similarly, for that sense of recognition which sets the heart beating can't be imagined.

Or can it?

Eventually, we were called down to join the gathering, just as I have always been called down, to and away from what has felt most significant. 'Supper's ready' – that tragic line in Robert Frost's poem 'Out, Out' – which leads to a child's death, was probably the message of the moment and, in its own way, was designed to cut short that chance for the soul, and the dangerous intimacy that goes with it, to blossom.

I have never slept with a woman.

There was one moment during my time at Sherborne that might arguably support the notion of the soul. It was one of the few occasions in my life when I reacted not to an instruction but to a call from within.

The occasion was a visit from a BBC journalist who came to interview sixth formers in our swanky new common room. A group of students was selected to answer questions. If Sherborne then was anything like the last school where I taught, they were probably picked for their enthusiasm and charm. A gaggle of them gathered around this man, who was short and insignificant-looking, rather as Iago should look insignificant – or would, if it were up to me to cast him.

Bunched together on stools, he asked if we thought the education at Sherborne better than in state schools. And whether it made us happy. They launched into a chorus of complaints. No, the teachers were useless, the school rules too strict, the uniform disgusting, the food the same, it was a waste of money...

I sat silently, uncomfortable and solemn, until a force made my face hot. 'It's a wonderful school,' I said, and I meant it. I knew what the others said was true. But I knew too how privileged we were and, more crucially, that this man had been sent to catch the sound of our queenly voices in a display of criticism which would only further his own political agenda.

Despite Sherborne's faults, the truth was that its traditions, its library, its atmosphere of scholarship made me the determined person I was, at least when I was a nun – even if I am lacking in ability or interest in matters that animate most people, such as the rights and wrongs of private schools, the ever-present problem of world hunger, whether one should be a vegan, an eco-warrior, a communist, an anything you care to think of that ends in an -ist.

Another more personal moment of objection to an adult's behaviour occurred when I was thirteen and at home. The family had visitors for supper: people with names like Audrey and Dick and Captain This, Field Marshal That. It was an occasion when all three children were expected to assist and be amusing on cue.

My mother had spent the afternoon juggling saucepans, boiling peas, instructing me to pick mint from the walled garden, poking potatoes, checking the state of the joint of lamb and rustling up gravy. Her pale blue eyeshadow began fading the moment it had been dabbed on, her big capable hands lashing out at dishes that refused to fit into their allocated spaces. Once at the table, she laughed loudly, her fang (the pointed molar that always provoked mirth in my father) flashing at Dick and Derek and Field Marshals This and That. My father was customarily well-oiled with gin in order to muddle through the challenge of conversation. Was it the drink that led to the evening's tactless blunder?

'Everyone sit down. John, please help! Make everyone sit down.'

'Sit down everyone.'

'Now Audrey, how many potatoes for you? Two? Is that all? What would you like, Derek? Perhaps easiest to help yourself then.'

'Much easier.' My father again, that fellow evader, at his best when things happened without him having to move.

But then – the mistake.

'So Bomby – (his nickname for me as a child) – 'tell us what you bought on your trip to the Great Metropolis?'

'Went to Woolworths.'

'And what did you buy in Woolworths?'

'An exercise book.'

All knives and forks down. Everyone looking. Because on the rare occasions that my father talked, either everyone listened. Or nobody did.

'And?'

'And some nail varnish.'

'What else?'

'Paper.'

'In Axworthy's?'

'Woolworths.'

'And?'

'I can't remember.'

My face grew hotter, everyone on me, and my father within touching, hugging, kicking distance, wildly urging the conversation on.

'Oh, come on, you must remember! What was it you actually bought?'

My body shot up and out of the room, up the stairs and into the big, cold spare room, which for some reason I was sleeping in that night. I climbed under the homemade orange-and-white floral bedspread and polycotton sheets and cried.

Downstairs, my mother threw all pretence of politeness to the winds: 'You stupid man! What did you do that for? You're the end. Go up and say sorry.'

So, up he came. Loose, long, thin legs, bumbling, humming and ha-ing. He sat gingerly on the side of the bed.

'Bomby…'

No answer.

'Sorry.'

Still no answer. I hated being angry with him but decided he deserved it.

'I didn't mean to upset you.'

I sat up, rumpled, wary.

My mother had taken me to buy my first bra that day.

The interrogation would have been bad enough in front of the family. In the presence of Audrey, Derek, Field Marshal this and Deaconess That, his behaviour was unforgiveable.

I love him for it now: the part of him that suddenly careers at speed, and then bang! He has flipped himself into a blunder.

I have followed much the same trajectory myself.

Many of the girls I knew at Sherborne are Ladies now, some attached to Lords, others to Field Marshals – Lady This of That, Lady That of This. After supper, as if in training for a wedding, all house members were required to line up in the housemistress's sitting room ready to shake her hand. Occasionally, if she had something to say, such as, 'You could do with a dash of deodorant' or 'Well done in your quadratic equations', she would whisper in your ear. Otherwise, it was a handshake so violent that as a small person, you always felt you needed a sit-down afterwards.

One such time, a girl called Hilary, older than me, plain, with a pasty face and black hair so solid it looked as if it had issued from a bottle, stood ahead of me in the queue. When she stuck out her hand to be shaken, it was grasped with such force that she collapsed in a lump. Everyone could see her underpants. We were shocked by the sight of a body on the blue carpet, dead as far as we could tell, but it got up and was led off to sickbay.

Another great waste of time and opportunity was when we had to return to our housemistress's living quarters once a week for what was called Drawing Room. This was an after-supper activity when we could have been reading a book, writing one even. Instead, we had to sit and talk about what was happening in the world, all the while doing a piece of needlework.

Needlework itself was a supreme waste of time. Now I envy those who can turn up their Field Marshal's hems, run up a dart, not to mention a dress or a pair of chinos for a Captain. At least needlework lessons had the right name. Now, it's called textiles, for which read sticking pieces of material in a scrapbook, a fine activity for a youngster. We, by contrast, had to make our own nightdresses. This took an entire school year, for the teacher was never available to help. But I wore the nightdress I made in that class for years afterwards. Its innocent sweetness would one day save me from a rape…

Uninterested in these evenings of nothingness, I often left my sewing behind. So, as one set of girls left, I would beg a piece of handiwork from one of the preceding set of victims. This would invariably be a blue art overall on which whoever it was had been pretending to sew her initials in white wobbly stitches, because she too had forgotten her needlework, if indeed she had any in the first place.

I talked enthusiastically in these sessions because, if you didn't, they were even more of a waste of time than if you did. One time, my housemistress told me off for going on so much, and 'Please would you close your legs, I can see your underpants.' In shock, I began sewing the blue overall to my skirt so that when I got up, it hung from my waist like a clinging friend.

My housemistress was never amused. In contrast, her protégées enjoyed the kind of laughter which gives as much pain as pleasure: the blue carpet, bay window, open fire, and the housemistress's fat legs all crashing and shattering inside them. I wished for only one thing more: my mother and the smell of my father's pipe, and his long thin legs collapsing into a chair, double-crossed.

Wherever I was, whether at school as a small girl, in India as a young adult, or in Kent as a try-it-out-for size grown-up, I knew exactly when he would be in his chair, smoking and swearing and slipping food to the dogs, alone with his God and his memories. We asked him before he died about the war. Again and again we asked, but he would say nothing other than that he regarded his time as Beach Master during the Normandy landings as his gap year. A year!

So, we persist: 'Weren't you miserable?'

'No.'

'Didn't it shock you seeing so many dead?'

No answer.

'What about being sent to boarding school when you were eight? Didn't that make you sad?'

'No.'

'Were you never homesick?'

'Not particularly.'

'Did you ever wish you had had brothers and sisters?'

'Not specially.'

'Are you in a bad mood, sad, not feeling great today?'
'Not really.'

For a person who said so little, he was one of the most interesting of men, and for no reason I can put into words. In some part of himself, he was un-grown, innocent and tactless, also uncomfortable with any vehicle that took him in the direction of London. That was a place he loathed, as he did anything which required him to be elsewhere, when all he wanted was to be here, 'in my chair'.

I was at home at the time of my mother's death on Christmas Eve. He was long and thin in his bed when I went in to tell him. He made a sound like a hyena, turned over and went back to sleep. Indeed, we both spent that day lying down, me in his dressing room, in the bed he had slept in as a child, while the shock of the snow outside and the death of our mother (for she was, in some way, his mother too) alone in a room in Totnes cottage hospital, sank in.

All day.

All the next day.

On and on, the snow wrapping the house in silence and weight.

THE INGENUE

Friends are like a sea with only an outward tide; unless you draw them in, they move further and further out. My closest friend at fifteen was Hoshi. Thanks to the nunnery's rule about detaching yourself from past friendships, I only have Hoshi by the thread of an annual Christmas card and, of late, a precious walk in Kew Gardens, where we took up where we had left off at sixteen.

At school, in the latter years, when I had become more interested in academic work, Hoshi was my daily companion. Trilingual and soon to be in possession of an Italian boyfriend, she loved roses and velvet and her essays were understated and clever, handwriting low to the line of the page and consistent. She was more exotic than beautiful, like her mother, who smoked heavily and drank black coffee. My mother drank only tea and smoked a single cigarette, which she lodged under her top lip, not inhaling as Hoshi's mother did – deeply.

Weekends at Hoshi's house in Bournemouth were sparkling treats. Arriving in December, we would be driven down streets full of Christmas lights whose beckoning was one of the high points of my youth. The streetlights were our lights, only ours, illuminating life away from the dreariness of the classroom.

Once she had learnt to drive, Hoshi would borrow her parents' car and, as soon as we arrived, we'd take a ride in the darkness to the beach and walk along the promenade. On these night walks, we talked about who God was, what and who we were, our conversation flowing so easily that afterwards we felt both rested and exhilarated.

On Saturdays, we would go to the ice rink, rent out white boots with important laces, hold hands and circle fast in a forward tilt to the sound of piped music. Then, high on the bus, we'd arrive home, delightfully chilled, having trawled the shops in the hope of something made of silk.

Sometimes we would pay Bunny a visit – the lunatic cousin with a passion for dirigibles, destined for a swanky grave behind gates and given only a cursory weeding each Christmas. He was a dear host, ensuring always, in readiness for our appetites or his own, a generous supply of cream cakes, the like of which I haven't seen for forty years. His house was dark and empty, but somehow exotic. If in the mood, he'd take us up to his attic and show us old films of balloons. As we watched the flickering screen, he would drone on in a deadly way that was comforting, for it made one feel that no serious effort was needed in life – one just had to be there, breathing in the strange air of a strange man's house that wasn't school.

At fifteen, unless a parent raised an objection, all pupils were confirmed. The lessons leading up to the event made God sound like a moderately decent civil servant who concealed his identity behind prayers, readings, rules and chants.

But it didn't stop us being excited.

Confirmation day itself was loaded with enchantments, some religious, others material. In the morning, we dressed in floral Viyella dresses with puffed sleeves and bodices, also raspberry-pink woollen knee socks, folded over twice.

After breakfast, there being no lessons, Hoshi and I went for a walk. We loved walking. It was on walks that, nobody seeming to care where we were, we indulged in companionable philosophising.

The confirmation walk ended in the park opposite my brother's boarding house, where we sat on a bench in what looked like a rundown bus shelter. There we talked about what would happen when the bishop touched our heads at the confirmation service. Why we thought this the right place for such a conversation I don't know. All I remember is the watching of people, and it being on that day that we concluded that all old people looked like tortoises. It was the way they held their heads at a horizontal to their necks; how they poked them out of their macintoshes or coats.

From the park, we went straight to the Abbey, a vast space that smelt of tapestry and moths – not that I have ever smelt a moth. We sat up straight and proud in the front pew, waiting for the service to start. When it did, with its customary catalogue of mundane announcements, there were too many hymns, and the sermon was as dull as every other in my childhood. Somewhere behind the vicar stood the bishop in his pointed hat, fiddling about with linen cloths and cups, like someone preparing for a dinner party. That is, perhaps, how our confirmation might have turned out, had God bothered to turn up.

On and on the whole business went, but our disposition was prone to joy, and all this waiting gave our excitement time to escalate. For surely, after all the dressing up, the cups, the silver, the velvet, the smell of incense and the chanting, even if God was otherwise engaged, *something* would happen when we went up and knelt at the altar rail.

Nope. Not a dicky bird. The bishop touched our heads, mumbled a few words along the lines of you are now welcomed into the church of Our Lord, the something of something, and we returned unmoved to our pews. Afterwards, we gathered in the nave and burst into tears – the best part of the proceedings, and entirely manufactured, to help us feel that something of importance had happened, even if it hadn't.

The most disappointing aspect of the day was the behaviour of my parents. Given that my father was in a black suit with pocket watch and reunited with his treasured gold cufflinks, and my mother in one of her important coats, I thought, at the least, they would be hushed and respectful. But all they did was to rush me out of the Abbey, into the car and straight to a local hotel where they enjoyed a large tea followed by an evening of prime-time television in a chintz-curtained room on the nylon ground floor.

It was on this day that I subconsciously dismissed my parents from my list of special people. Now that they are gone, they are remembered daily, nightly, morning after morning. At one of their funerals, my brother summed it up, saying that as parents they had given their children stability. Though that word would have filled Hoshi and me with derision when we were sixteen, I now rate the quality highly. Too much intensity is no good thing for an over-thinker.

Part of the privilege of a stable childhood was the ease with which we moved from one experience to another. When at five, seven and nine, respectively, on the sunny beach of Dawlish, we saw a dead body, bloated and white, bobbing its way towards us as we splashed in the shallows, we simply allowed ourselves to be shepherded behind a rock, where our mother distracted us with a game called *Guess the Tune by the Taps I Make on this Rock*. Our father, meanwhile, called upon his naval training and organised the men in his midst to pull the body out. And that was that. On with the swimming, the sandwiches, the drive home.

I was similarly matter-of-a-fact at school. I had just given myself to God. He/she had shown no interest, despite my badgering him/her nightly with requests and promises. But I was loyal, rising early each Sunday to look for him/her in Sherborne Abbey, instinct telling me that God was more likely to be around at the early service than the one after breakfast. This was an assumption later confirmed in the nunnery, for there we rose at four, sometimes as early as two. But when nothing happened, I turned back to Balzac. And moments later, I was in France.

It was the spring of 1974 when they told me I was going to Nantes for three weeks to learn to speak 'like a native' (my father). I was sixteen and newly initiated to the sixth form. Mrs Gill, the small passionate woman whom I longed to know as a human being, had chosen my host family, and my parents trusted the school to make appropriate arrangements, as did I.

The selected girl, Marianne, introduced herself by sending a photo with a short letter in that curlicue script so enviable in French handwriting. The picture must have been taken by her photographer brother for it was set on the diagonal and signed as if by the film star it seemed to depict. When I held it up for study one morning at breakfast, my brother snatched it and kept it to himself for several nights in a row while I dutifully wrote back. My tone was awkward and monotonous, a default mode of expression adopted when a nasty experience is felt to be looming.

On arrival in Nantes, the first port of call was the house of Marianne's mother, a person with a frightening grey crew cut. All my life I had lived with a woman with a perm, friendly hats made of plastic petals or a headscarf. This female was, in contrast, divorced, modern, an academic, feminist, structuralist, post-structuralist even. Definitely not, by instinct, a mother, which was perhaps, I later deduced, why her daughter was so sophisticated.

No sooner had I arrived than, without so much as a biscuit, we were whisked off to a large villa where Marianne's father spent the summer with his four sons. The main building was laid out in a horseshoe design with a swimming pool in the middle. Everyone was treated to poolside quarters with French windows, a common-enough arrangement now, but ahead of its time then, and, for its stink of money, unnerving.

On this next arrival, I was taken to my room, which also had its own en-suite bathroom before such things were invented in my world.

The person in Nantes who showed me to my room, informed me in none too friendly a tone that I was to be unpacked and in the dining room by seven. There was no explanation as to where the dining room might be. At sixteen, I hadn't learnt the self-protective habit I later adopted when arriving in any unfamiliar bedroom, which is to lay out my possessions in such a way as to make the room mine, so it will welcome me back on my return to sleep. Instead, confused and afraid, I left my case where it was, went into the bathroom, looked at myself in the mirror, walked about, then, still dressed in the green jersey bell-bottoms I had worn for travel (trousers of the kind my mother wore in her mid-eighties), made several wrong turnings before finding the destination.

Late.

I have always been late.

The dining room was an enormous space, so defined by glass that I walked straight into a window, smashing my forehead. Even that nasty little shock to my confidence was as nothing compared to what next greeted my eyes: a small man seated very much at the head of 'my huge table, in my huge house'. Like his ex-wife, he was grey-haired and, had he been dressed, would no doubt have also been got up in leather. Instead, he was wearing a striped kimono which hung open to reveal his naked body. Most prominent, for it being my first view, was that prune-like appendage that I had no word for then, having never had to name such a thing in the normal run of life.

With him at the table were four young men (clothed), all at least eight years older than me, and the beautiful

Marianne who was dressed in some kind of exotic combination of denim and pink. My first reaction to the father was to think he must be a criminal. Nowadays, I often walk about my own house with nothing on. But this is a recent habit, a reaction against the constraints of living as either nun or child. The very thought of a naked man at a meal seemed to me, then, the height of immorality. My confusion redoubled when lobster was served, a dish whose complications I have since avoided.

Not long after dinner, Monsieur flung off his kimono and jumped into the pool with a proprietorial splash.

Marianne appears in my head only as she was in her bedroom on another day, when she was showing me the contents of her wardrobe. There was nothing flashy or unpleasant about her. She had the poise and understatement of the classy girl, whereas I was still 'gay, frank and open' (a quote from my house report of 1974); a giggly person wanting only the womb-like warmth of a Devonshire summer.

I recall only one statement Marianne made over the course of those three weeks: 'Attention! Mon frère est méchant.' The trouble with 'son frère' was that he was also irresistible: dark-haired, strong, confident and – crucially – old. Twenty-four to my sixteen and attracted perhaps to... what? My Englishness?

One evening, after another long supper, he, Marianne and a couple of her other siblings were playing cards, when he slipped a note across the wooden floor in my direction.

Plus tard dans ta chambre.

Just as I did thirty years later, when a quack physician in Amsterdam told me that my insomnia was due to a worm in my brain, and that by mere touch he had removed it, my heart started up a fast beat and I felt as if, in the space of a second, I had achieved all that I would ever want in life. He, this film star of a person, was wanting to do things to me that no other had done, though a few had tried.

But I had always run away.

It wasn't until late that evening that I heard a tap on my window. Fight, flight, freeze. The three shock reactions – perhaps fawning came later? – wheeled out by the experts. No chance of the first unless I punched him on the nose. Flight wasn't possible. So – freeze! Stand still, in the crimson acrylic nightdress, another of those unfortunate Christmas presents that set my hair ablaze. Then a long-suspended moment when my body gave no signal. Wasn't even present. Just the crimson and the fire and the sound of knuckles.

Insistent now.

To be factual about it, the response that followed is typical of both a reckless and fatalistic side of my personality, in that I finally gave up.

Let him in.

Not quite into my body.

But into the room.

I can see his face now. Those wide lips, olive skin, black hair. Nothing of his body. Nothing of mine. Only a memory of limbs involved with each other. Clumsiness on his part. No words, no affection.

Fumbling.

When he left the room, I went into the bathroom, looked once more in the mirror and saw a stranger, crumpled, crooked, ugly and unclean. He had disarranged my hair as well as my being, in the way that only wrong touch can.

I have learnt since that if someone who loves you touches you, and then you look in the mirror, you can appear to yourself to be different. I have subjective proof. After one such encounter, I visited my elderly aunt who was days away from dying, in a home in Somerset. When she saw who it was, she said, 'I'm so glad you're beautiful.' She was so glad I was loved, for only love had performed this brief transformation.

The next day, Marianne having disappeared as she did throughout my stay, her brother asked if I'd fancy a drive. I knew I should say no but I said yes, watching with awe as he slung a large camera with zoom lens over his shoulder and opened the passenger door. I didn't trouble to ask where we were going. In front of a gate he made me stand while he took multiple snaps, then drove me to a block of high-rise flats.

Inside the small dark box of a lift, I felt the heat of his presence. Shaking with joy, I thought that he was going to kiss me. And then there he was, doing just that, his great face squelching and squeezing and smelling of leather. My own face was hot and red, for there was no doubt in my mind that he was now in love with me.

Writing this now, I begin to wonder if the kiss in the lift didn't happen before the tumble in the bedroom, for surely after that, a kiss in a lift wouldn't have made such an impression.

But there is something about a lift...

Four days before the end of the holiday, which had been far too long, we returned to the leather mother's leather house. There I spent days unsupervised in a bedroom, nursing a stomach ache and reading a French novel about a drug addict called Sophie. I have no recollection of meals, of anyone else in the vicinity, or any organised activity, apart from the night when the leather son barged into my bedroom while I was half asleep. There was a nasty edge to him as he approached, pulled back the bedding and, progressing from mere fumbling, rammed his finger up my vagina. Having known the hands of two doctors in search of orifices, I mentally absented myself from this moment of intrusion and took refuge inside the tent of my home-made blue and white nightdress. (I had thrown the crimson, acrylic nightdress into a nearby bin.) Perhaps those fraught Sherborne sewing lessons which had produced a less than elegant garment had worked their magic? This is how I tend to think of events that have been troubling – that they were meant to be, but were prevented, and no real harm was done.

Or was there? I am still afraid of kissing. Of intimacy, entangled limbs, bed-sharing…

My last encounter with 'that bloody frog' (my father) was a couple of days before I came home. He had invited me to a gymkhana, which I would normally have avoided for I have little affinity with horses. I was aware of his cooled interest and did not investigate my own. A light had gone out and the air had become thin. Blankly, I pulled on the green jersey trousers again, and the brown T-shirt. He, an historical sex offender who, if still knocking about the planet, must be in his mid-seventies now, drove me, camera slung once more cockily around his neck, until we reached a rambling park. And here zenith's antonym occurred when – oh, let's call him François – strode straight up to a girl who looked like the Duchess of Cambridge and embraced her with the respect and tenderness of a medieval knight.

That evening, I evaded all formal proceedings and walked out of the mother's house, down the road towards some nearby marshland in search of pathetic fallacy, a phrase my students have difficulty weaving into a sentence. With me, I dragged some fellow who was hanging around since the return to the mother's house. I had no idea who he was, but I sensed he was one of life's victims. For all I know, he might be Monsieur Sarkozy, or the co-prince of Andorra, by now.

Seated on a boulder, I tried telling him that I longed to telephone my parents to fetch me. But the words wouldn't come, for my parents wouldn't have dreamt of setting foot in France and would never have approved of a change of plan.

But I was desperate. Sadder than ever before. François was stuck in my head like a growth. All I could see was him kissing his horsey princess. And all I could feel was the relief it would be to stand once more beside my mother, stirring bread sauce.

Back home, I was marched around Torquay, past the Pavilion Theatre, close to the harbour, then asked in faux-nonchalant tones: 'Are you still a virgin?' I gave my mother only a tremulous: 'Might be, might not be.'

She was furious. You can't have it both ways was my reasoning. If your mother takes no interest in rescuing you from endless exiles in dangerous places, then she has no right to be in on your secrets. But my real anger was about my teeth, my breasts, my clothes and beautiful Marianne in her beautifully cut jeans. As for the twenty-four-year-old François and would-be rapist, I knew him for a cad, and I was still in love with him. And that, as far as I was concerned, was my mother's fault.

RECOVERY

The next term, I was appointed head of house. This meant that, instead of sleeping in a cubicle, I had a room to myself. But I was unwell; I looked and felt jaundiced. Finally, without any queues, matrons, or uppish doctors with eager fingers, I was sent home where I stayed until Christmas.

For six to eight weeks, a green acrylic hat and winceyette pyjamas were my daily rig as I sat on the sofa reading. This might seem a justifiable response to a bout of ill-health but one of Yarde's unspoken rules was that you were not to sit on a sofa until after lunch or ever be visible in nightwear downstairs.

My mother's doctor pronounced glandular fever. I was relieved to be labelled while I knew I wasn't in fact physically ill. François hadn't quite taken my virginity, but he and his family had taken something else which was never fully regained. And whatever was left of that precious quality – innocence, perhaps – was, in the end, donated to the nunnery.

After a month on the sofa, my mother finally imposed herself upon someone by the name of Munro, a Canadian with long white hair, who lived alone in a house that overlooked the River Dart. He smelt of polos and taught

Latin, a subject I loved. So, side by side, Munro and I moseyed through *The Aeneid*. As I began to recover, by the fire, on the beach – 'Breathe, go on, sea air will do you good!' – I wrote speeches in the style of Cicero and Tacitus, in the hope of impressing the beautiful, young Latin master who never marked our work.

Then my brother came home and with him the vitality that has characterised each of his sixty-eight years. He was in his first year at Dartmouth Naval College and I was to go with him and his friends to a ball. The boy I wanted to shepherd me was a plumpish, innocuous fellow with trustworthy fingers; he lived on the Isle of Mull and was religious; he also had his eye on my much more suitable sister.

Dressing up in some concoction of pink and cream brought my body back to me – that's the great thing about clothes – for, in the weeks with Munro on the sofa, I felt it had wandered out of reach. Now it was back, I wanted not only to dance but to go back to school, to walk once more with Hoshi, talk with Hoshi, sit high in the library, write essays and be returned to the rigour which, despite its shortage of decent teachers, was the chief virtue of Sherborne, and one that the fellow from the BBC was determined to ignore.

Finally began what was called the seventh term, when Hoshi and I were exempt from the more boring aspects of school life and allowed to do as we wished. Most days were spent in the library, a dark-panelled cathedral at the top of the main school building. There I waded through *Clarissa* and *Tom Jones*; then came up with a theory about all fine literature posing questions rather than answering them, which I must have copied from a critic but adopted as my own. It began with Virginia Woolf's little novel *Between the Acts*, then Chekhov's short stories, Katherine Mansfield, a novel by Turgenev, Balzac...

In December, having sat the entrance exam to Oxford – cheek laid against the desk, pen held at an angle in my left hand, rambling peaceably about enjambments and caesuras – I was summoned for an interview.

The little college bedroom was like a slightly upgraded boarding school room. And the dining room had that essential capacity to merge with another – Westwing – for they both had top tables. Then there was the junior common room where all interviewees were to wait. Surveying my rivals happily, I wasn't in the least concerned that they might be chosen ahead of me, because I had been well briefed for failure. 'We don't think you should apply for Oxbridge; you'd be very unlikely to get in'. But I had already got in. Here I was, inside the college, seated among the bright and the beautiful.

The first interview was conducted by a minuscule person whose feet, when she was settled in her plush blue armchair beside an open fire, didn't quite reach the floor. She asked no questions; didn't, for example, unnerve me with cruel spatial awareness tests such as: 'If the door is behind you and the window is to your left how many oranges would be in your bag?' Nor did she ask about the architecture of Oxford, of which I knew nothing. Instead, she left me free to go on about the sprung rhythm of Gerard Manley Hopkins, then on to Chekhov, Anouilh, Katherine

Mansfield and the much-in-vogue Virginia Woolf... On and on I went, forgetting Hoshi's coolness, oozing childlike eagerness, while my listener sat peacefully twisting her arthritic fingers in her lap. There seemed to be no definitive end to the interview, which was the nub of my thesis – that important things have no firm conclusion. (Discuss.)

For the second interview, I was taken to the principal's study, a huge room which, by way of furniture, had only an old brown sofa. Before me was a strange-looking person of indeterminate gender and no hair, apart from a couple of bewitching tufts that seemed to issue from his/her/their ears. Present for the meeting was also a one-eyed dog. The talk was a light brush over Wordsworth, a poet I had grown to dislike, having read of how badly he betrayed his friend, the greater genius, Coleridge. I had also drummed up some interest in his flawed philosophy from the preface to *Lyrical Ballads*.

By the middle of December, I had left Sherborne. The last day is vivid, only insofar as it involved a summons to the headmistress's study. I had expected nothing from the meeting beyond the formality of a handshake. So, when I left her room and was walking the long corridor towards the cloakrooms, I was surprised to find that I was shaking. For at the end of the meeting, the headmistress had stared at me and said: 'You have something special to do'. Inside, my head said: 'Yes I know.'

Had she divined something of my future? Was she referring to the nunnery I joined in 1980? Being fiercely religious, she would have approved of that, despite it being based in India.

Or maybe I have all this wrong. My dear friend Hoshi recently told me that, by the time we left school, the big-bosomed headmistress of my memory had herself already left. The new headmistress, a decent but not noteworthy person, was not given to eye-talking.

As always, everything was swiftly forgotten on return to Devon. Back in the delightful company of my friend and fellow partygoer, Loo Brown, I now went up to London on a Christmas shopping trip. After Hoshi, Loo was one of my two best friends from home – a compulsive giggler with no subtext, no hang-ups about God or the universe and its maker. Loo was about boys, roll-up cigarettes, splashing about naked in the Aegean and fooling her elderly parents into thinking she was in one place, when she was in another, usually in bed with a boy. Her father, Dr Brown, didn't live up to the surname he shared with my childhood maths teacher, though he was the gentlest of men, much liked by my mother.

In London, we spent the day rifling through the cheap and cheerful treasures of Carnaby Street or somewhere, at least, where you could buy crimson loons and tight T-shirts, then on to Biba, the best clothes shop in the land, for it sold sombre dresses cut (at last!) from good cloth.

Travelling back to Newton Abbot on the milk train, we lay among sacks of post, chattering and snoozing and fidgeting, then stomped up the hill and straight into the clean sheets of the Browns's spare room.

Early the same morning, Mrs Brown came to the bedroom door. How gentle her voice! A milk-and- biscuits voice.

'The phone. For you.'

There being no such thing as cordless phones then, I must have gone downstairs to discover the mystery caller.

'You've got into Oxford.'

I wasn't particularly moved by my father's announcement. But I always seem to be neutral in the face of big-deal news. In fact, the more big-deal it is, the bigger the blank, as if my mind knows it must keep the information for later. This is a weakness, for, often when the reaction does kick in, the original event has long passed and I am thus troubled by attacks of unprompted fury.

Perhaps my parents are partly to blame. When the girls I now teach receive good exam results, they are hugged, photographed and taken out for meals. At worst, treated to new clothes, cars or cash. But on my arrival back at Yarde nothing of a celebratory nature followed: no gifts, no alcohol consumed. And champagne was, anyway, strictly reserved for toasting the Queen. But, surely, they must have been pleased?

Looking back, I feel what seemed to be lacking was the kind of rational conversation in which an intelligent adult sits you down and gently shakes you into the present by talking through what has just happened, and discussing what might happen next. My parents never did this; nor did I expect them to. Events simply rolled on.

And the next event, designed, possibly, to help me grow up, involved another exile – 'we think it a treat'. I was to spend six months in a place, conjured out of nowhere it seemed, as being the most distant possible location to which I might usefully be banished.

'*Australia*?'

'You leave in three weeks.'

'Why am I being sent away again?'

'I don't know.'

It was the day before my departure. I was sitting on my bed, suitcase half-packed. The question blurted out, and my mother was suddenly as close to tears as I ever saw her.

But it was too late. The plane was booked, arrangements made with a shooting friend of my father's, a Colonel Somebody-or-Another, who had agreed to contact his sister who lived in Sydney: 'Of course you can stay with her. It would be her pleasure'. After which I was to move on to Adelaide to look after two children of a woman who was the cousin of another Lord Somebody-of-Somewhere.

It was a long journey, with a stop in Kuala Lumpur where the package deal included a three-night stay in the Hilton hotel. As in France, it is the lift I remember most vividly. I have no recollection of the bedroom I slept in, but going up and down in that mobile silver box somehow encapsulated the shocking sense of loneliness I felt during these endless days, for I had never before been to a hotel alone.

On the first night of my stay in Sydney with Lady X of Y, I drew the bedroom curtains so hard that the curtain rail fell down.

'Well, that's a pain. Why did you do that?'

I was shocked by my hostess's wording, as well as her candour. She was English. She should at least pretend to be nice. As a nun, I developed a kind of reverence for physical objects, investing them with significance – an attitude which, if odd, at least prevented me from causing accidents. As a child, however, I had been both clumsy and untidy, the victim of quicksilver emotions that seemed to make things – furniture, doors, cupboards, now curtains – unduly vulnerable to my handling. A wisecrack psycho-babbler might suggest that causing damage was my way of gaining attention. In Sydney, the tactic had no such effect.

'You just sit here by the swimming pool and later I'll take you to my club for lunch.'

I had never heard of anyone having a club. I thought it must be related in some way to sewing, shooting or, at the very least, sport. Instead, it involved a gaggle of ladies in pink lipstick, long shorts and dyed blonde hair who gathered to talk.

I was glad to leave Lady X and fly to a large ranch-style bungalow in Adelaide. Here, I came upon my employer, dressed in a pink knee-length housecoat and matching mules, putting out the rubbish. Most of the things I found shocking as a child, I now habitually do myself. Putting out the rubbish in my nightwear being one of them. But at the time, I formed the view that she must be immoral and not to be trusted. She turned out, in fact, to be supremely kind, as well as immoral – for which read relaxed. In the six months I was with her, I was kissed by at least fifteen boys, learnt jazz dancing, sunbathed naked, drank vodka and began to swear. I also became pleasantly plump, didn't read a single book, stopped caring about the universe and who made it or why, and ate a lot of steak.

Here again I observe that, when unhappy, passivity is generally my response. In this case, it was back to Sydney, to a motel, a water park, a coach journey to Alice Springs and Darwin, a long drive through Victoria, a weekend on Kangaroo Island, where I shared a bunk bed with a solidly good-looking blonde, and a Land Rover ride over some dunes.

There was no full-blown sex in Australia, although I was ready for it, and was in and out of bed with many a youth. But it always stopped short, and I am grateful for that now. Think, for example, what a shame it would have been to be de-flowered by a coach driver, who looked a little like the actor Alan Bates and was in charge of a three-week journey to Alice Springs and the Northern Territories.

When, in late summer, fuelled by meat and alcohol, I returned to Devon, I was a stone fatter, firmly stationed in my body and no longer interested in God or similes. Keen to capture me in this question-free state, my father arranged a photographer to shoot (!) me on the lawn – soon to be denuded of its apple tree to accommodate a marquee for my sister's wedding. I dislike that photo now: the unplucked eyebrows, the hint of spots and the vulgar hooped earrings. Others think it flattering, apart from one friend, whose soul knows my own and whose comment is rather: 'I like you better as you are now. There's something missing in that picture.'

THE FOLLOWER

Ann Wordsworth was my first tutor at Oxford and the epitome of all that was bad. I was surprised, relieved even then, to read of her death a few years ago in the St Hugh's magazine, where she was described as a kindly woman who loved her garden.

Just as the tutor who interviewed me seemed rooted for life to her chair, legs dangling, Ann Wordsworth seemed for all time to be stationed in a small shed. To reach this odd, almost touching little building, students had to make their way through a garden, open the shed door, walk through a minuscule room with a single bed into an even tinier room with an electric fire. On this fire, throughout each tutorial, AW lit up, sucked on and stubbed out one Gauloise cigarette after another.

The first time I made this perilous journey, there was half an avocado pear on Ms Wordsworth's pillow. I was shocked. But, as with the warm-hearted Australian who took out her rubbish in a dressing gown, I have graduated to eating an avocado in bed during my later life.

'Hello.'
'Yes?'

'My essay on *Wuthering Heights*.'

'Yes.'

Head low. Black wavy hair, small teeth, not unlike the little false ones of Brown Owl's daughter that I had dropped down the drain at primary school.

'What should I do with it?'

'Read it out.' As if I should know this was what one did, when all my academic life I had handed in work to be returned and marked. Still, I had attended lessons in elocution throughout school years, reciting poems to a spinster with large lips who sipped sherry as she listened. I had also taken exams in speechmaking so I wasn't as nervous as I would be now; I can't even read a page of a novel out loud to a class without feeling I might need CPR.

Quiet voice: 'I love *Wuthering Heights*. It is the most passionate love story between two people who are affined by soul, heart not class, and first meet when –'

'Stop!'

I look up, hurt.

AW sucks on the Gauloise, head low, eyes hidden by a long fringe. Then announces that there are no people in *Wuthering Heights*.'

'Aren't there?'

And in a gently menacing monotone, à la Roland Barthes (who, I learnt only recently, died about a day before he tried to write a novel himself): 'We're not interested in characterisation.'

Who was *we*?

'What you need to write about is the precursor to *Wuthering Heights*, the fact that it is a product of, transgressor, post precursor, the signifier of something-something-something…'

Quickly, I began taking note of the obscure lingo, not bothering to look the words up, but recycling them, flourishing them…

'That's better. That's a very sound essay.'

I was summoned at the end of the first year.

'We're thinking of giving you an Exhibition. Your essays have been so promising. We suggest you enter this essay-writing competition and we'll go from there.'

I chose to write about the different representations in art, literature and music of Mazeppa, who (Wikipedia says) was a Ukrainian called Ivan born in 1639. According to Byron's version of things, the young Mazeppa has a love affair with a Countess Theresa while serving as a page at the Court of King John II Casimir Vasa. On discovering the affair, the Countess's husband punishes Mazeppa by tying him naked to a wild horse.

Though bored now from copying out Wiki's useful summary, I can see why I might at the time have been drawn to this kind of storyline, having a couple of years earlier been rapt by a production of *Equus*. The problem, however, was that nobody had written an essay on Mazeppa, let alone multiple Mazeppas, so there was no critic to copy.

Soon, the appointed tutor was as bored with the essay as I was. I was not awarded the Exhibition, though some mention made it into a reference for a teaching post, handwritten some time later by Professor Marilyn Butler, also deceased.

Marilyn was my tutor in the second year and, being a pluralist, her tutorials lacked charge. She had a friendly bland face. Like a victim of a hideous regime to which I had become attuned, I found her kindness dull, as was her dog, which lay sprawled at all times under her desk. What I needed, or thought that I needed, was another enchanter, who (note) didn't have to be male but had to possess a daunting level of intelligence matched by a wealth of self-belief. The trouble with Butler, also central to her virtue as a teacher, was that she wanted to know what her students thought. But this student, at least, didn't think anything; only had vague sensations and physical yearnings. I hadn't read the Shakespeare, the Dickens (a week allocated for each), the Austen (on whom Butler was an expert), the Smollett, the Trollope... Reading took too long and I was too busy. As a consequence, what I wrote was dull, and what I said even duller.

Thanks to Marilyn Butler's mildness, I and my dear friend and fellow student, Adriana, smoked more Gauloises in The Eagle and Child pub and talked about 'It' – 'It' being God. We also puzzled over who the writer was since the writer, so we had been told in our first year, was said not to exist or if (s)he did, (s)he was merely a product of a mix of multiple societal influences. Thus, in a year, the stability of my childhood, in which each person, each place had a fixed preciousness and role, was shattered.

While Adriana had suffered a more complicated young life, she too felt this way. And so together, we clung to questions about ourselves as fixed entities. Who are we? What is the soul? Is there really a lobe in the brain dedicated to understanding metaphor? And all kinds of other Hoshinessess that provided us with a sense of security which so many grown people I now know seem not to need.

Hoshi, meanwhile, was in Edinburgh studying one, two, three of the multiple languages she could speak. She should have been with us at Oxford; she was certainly cleverer than all of us.

Adriana had the most extraordinary smile and was prone to bouts of heart-wrenching laughter. And, while Hoshi seemed to confine essential questions to the cerebral, Adriana and I took them into our hearts. We thought, lived, ate together, and often wore identical dresses in green and brown printed cheesecloth. I also emulated another friend, Chantal, who was extremely beautiful: small breasts, straight back, white teeth, black wavy hair and the owner of a startling pair of emerald-green lace-up boots. She had a long flowing cloak that billowed behind her as she rode her bicycle along Cowley Road. I borrowed it now and then, because it felt as though Chantal's clothes might invest me with sex appeal, a phrase, like inferiority complex, that I haven't heard for roughly half a century.

Having answers neither to the meaning of life, to ourselves nor the reason for such a lack of interesting boys, Adriana and I wandered around Oxford market where, to cheer ourselves up, we bought second-hand clothes. My favourite was a cheesecloth sack of a dress in cornflower blue.

One day we encountered a pouchy-faced psychometrist sitting on a stool near the market entrance. Now they are everywhere, the psychics and mystics, at the end of any phone line for a tenner an insight. I recently booked myself in with one who looks like an amalgam of Melania Trump and a middle-aged Spice Girl. In the mid-seventies of my conventional world, such rogues provided useful ego boosts, which came in the form of exciting predictions.

So, there we hovered, watching, as members of the crowd handed the psychometrist a piece of jewellery, a lock of hair or clothing, and were given in return a reading. Finally, the crowd dispersed and only we were left.

'Shall we? How much is it?'

So urgently were we in search of both stability and magic that we handed over our jewellery as well as our judgement. The readings satisfied our gullible conviction that we were special. Adriana's was full of well-deserved compliments, while I was told that I needed more green vegetables and should never eat standing up. The reading closed with the ominous words: 'You will sing a song of joy and a song of sorrow.' As we fumbled with our purses, the psychometrist served up her pièce de resistance: 'You are, both of you, as valuable as diamonds.'

Chuffed by the compliment, Adriana became a convert and made monthly trips to consult the psychometrist. For me it was a one-off. Perhaps reading *Macbeth* at school had alerted me to the danger of relying on witches' predictions; whereas Adriana had treated the play as a 'construct, that's right it's just a signifier' (whatever that is?). Or perhaps my reluctance was because the possession I handed over was the ring I had all but stolen as a child from my brother's godmother?

In those days, a poster was delivered daily to each college, listing available activities: plays, debates, science experiments, visiting poets. It also contained adverts for demonstrations of activities, such as the ancient Chinese art of T'ai Chi. I attended a promotion for that, and found it funny for no good reason other than that the pasty lady demonstrator sported a Japanese jumpsuit and talked about the eyes of a tiger. My provincialism still embarrasses me even now; I wish I had taken up T'ai Chi for the discipline might have stabilised me.

In the same daily poster I saw an advert for lessons with Kofi Annan who was not called that, of course, but Kofi was his first name and they didn't look dissimilar. He lived just up the road from St Hugh's. I was still looking for the stillness and magic of 'It', but 'It' had become more complicated, for I had gone beyond the spiritual and picked up a further theme: health. Yoga must be the answer. So, I went to the house and by chance found Kofi in his garden.

'Do you teach yoga?'

'I do.'

'Can I come to your lessons?'

Maybe I asked a different question, for his response seems like the kind of non-sequitur with which I have so often been met, and which my students at school also tend to come up with when bored.

'What you should do,' he said, 'is eat broccoli. Raw.'

I was cross. It was an answer which translated into 'Go away when I'm alone in my garden'. It was also an answer which meant 'stop asking about life and just get on with living it.'

But I couldn't *get on* because something was missing. And the missing something provoked a great sob in my soul.

The reason for my sadness? My intense yearning to find God and to lose my virginity. On both counts, it had been quite a long enough wait, as far as I was concerned. And finally, I had met a boy whom I shall call Quentin. He had jet-black hair, a blocked nose, child-smooth skin and, for uncertain reasons, it was he with whom I wished to share this rite of passage.

In those days, you could write to someone in another college and your letter would be delivered to their pigeonhole, a tradition which has doubtless been replaced by texting, sexting, tiktokking... However, all the most important letters I have received in my life have arrived in pigeonholes. And between Quentin and me there had been an enticing, if brief, correspondence, his letters particularly appealing for being written in green ink.

At the time, he was already going out with a girl in my year at St Hugh's, and for this reason he instructed me that we shouldn't meet for a month. One night, I decided to ignore his ruling and rode to his college on my psychedelic bicycle.

The room was square and imposing and there he was, lolling in front of a real log fire. When we kissed, it was one of the most exciting moments of my young life. Only after the kiss, were we an 'it'. And being an 'it' meant, if only temporarily, I stopped going on about the 'Great It', God and who (s)he was and who the author, what the book... Everything stopped because there in front of me was a lover. However, God had to come into it again as (s)he has all my life.

His letter. I wish I still had it, the one which went something to the effect that 'I want to sleep with you, but God says no.'

By this time, I was annoyed with God. He had made no effort. Not shown up at school, at confirmation, at communion, in conversation, anywhere... So why should he stand between me and my de-flowering?

As I wrote yesterday, we can't do it *because of God*.

I wrote back asking why not just get on with it; God surely had better things to do with his time than interfere with an individual's bodily pleasures?

At last, he agreed.

Whether Quentin had 'done it' before I had no idea. Perhaps not, for if he had then why did he fear making God cross? In the end, we did get it over with. The lights being turned off, I saw nothing of the event. I only remember it hurting. Worse was the fact that, when I woke the next morning, Quentin had disappeared. So, I got up and, putting on one of his jumpers, walked into his sitting room, buttered a smashed-up Matzo, smeared it with homemade marmalade and waited.

Evening: 'Where have you been?'

'On a sponsored walk.'

'Why didn't you tell me?'

Mumble, mumble. (Something to do with having to pay for his sin).

Oddly enough, I had suffered a strange experience myself on awakening in his narrow bed: a voice as real as the one I had heard in the headmistress's study at school, speaking straight into my head.

God is crying.

It was then that I thought he might have been right about it being the wrong thing to do.

The relationship with Quentin lasted an impressive nine months. In the end, his flashing around town in a black cloak, singing operatically in public and making grand gestures of affection began to jar. He came to stay with my family in Devon at least twice, and my father took to him warmly. Perhaps he knew he was rich or thought him funny? Or he simply felt drawn to him. For Quentin was still so much the child, in the way my father was a child, though he also had a vicious line in sniffing out unsuitable lovers. When, in my forties, I was dallying with an American egotist, my father sat me down and asked if I liked second-hand cars.

'Not much.'

'So don't go for one then.'

'Yeah, well you try meeting a man over forty who isn't second-hand!'

My father had no response.

Looking back, it seems unfair to dismiss Quentin as being merely ostentatious and uninterested in the big questions, for it was he who had raised the business of God. And I who had dismissed it in favour of my carnal needs. Later, too, the big questions consumed him so much that he went off to foreign parts and became some kind of priest.

But.

A thread that ran through Oxford and beyond, was the but. The *but* of who I actually was, and forever would be. Again and again, it kept surfacing like a night terror. During my first sexual encounter, fed up with the complications it caused, I had thrown it to the winds. But it kept slapping me in the face, as if demanding of me a seriousness which, in a reaction against the fractured life of modernism (Pablo Picasso would have terrified!), I both yearned for and wanted to avoid. I was young, agile, ambitious, interested in movement. Yet, as my tutor Ann Wordsworth might have commented: 'Your problem is that you have a regressive longing for a childhood which, for some, is when everything appears to have a fixed value.' Those *some* are protected and then shocked; those mysterious others are either shocked and shocked again or rush, shocked, straight into maturity.

It seems to me now, in an explanation which soothes and so is probably in itself a further sign of regression, that it is all to do with having an old soul in a young body. The old cries out for truth, while the child is only after pleasure. I have reminisced with others who studied at Oxford: those who found both their faith and their spouses during their three years among the spires. They're the ones who have families and dogs and a shared understanding of what matters. They tend to live in large houses, run church choirs and book clubs and do both weekly things and Sunday things and, unlike me, have no need to cancel engagements nor take sudden strange detours. In other words, they have gone for being fixed.

Not me.

To complement the charade that was Oxford, I gravitated towards acting. Capsized dramatically as to the question of who or what the self was, I had always liked pretending to be other selves. Blessed with a stronger nervous system, I might have made a reasonable character actress, though

I would never have been any good at learning lines. Why? Perhaps it's all part of a propensity for cheating, copying down the essays of critics rather than learning the text itself? Or it's a fault in my processing system, not unlike that suffered by so many pupils in my former workplace who seemed to benefit from diagnoses of malfunctions in their brains affording them an extra half hour in public exams and, for some, the chance for a lie-down midway through the ordeal.

Acting at Oxford was about the pleasure of rehearsals. These, not the play itself, were the real drama. Hanging around in halls, participants would burst into tears, smoke roll-ups, celebrate complexity; be by turns aloof, gushing, provocative, indirect... A boy we shall name Nick, who seemed to direct every play I was in, was dead keen on the high drama of emotion. With his encouragement, I learnt to manufacture strong feelings, conjure tears and so succeed in attracting the attention I'd been seeking since childhood.

Nick had a beard and spittle which, like Brown Owl's, collected at the corners of his mouth when he was excited; he also had an enviably beautiful girlfriend whom I wished to be, not because I liked him but because I liked her. Small, neat, dark and oriental, she epitomised my idea of beauty, which was everything I reckoned my family wasn't.

Once, at the beginning of a rehearsal, Nick told his assembled cast that the previous night he had urinated in the washbasin in his college bedroom. This set me against him for, despite my cavalier nature, I was always put off by laddish behaviour. Twenty years later, I saw him in a supermarket in Kilburn. I was in my nun's white habit, he in khaki trousers and a T-shirt, carrying a wire basket. Once more, I performed my evading act and hid behind a revolving newspaper stand. For what to say about who I had been and whom I had now become?

My undiscerning memory, typically, remembers the girl and the urinating anecdote but nothing much about the plays we performed. There was one in which I wore a black and white bonnet, and another staged in Magdalen Deer Park, where my second and rather important boyfriend studied. I played a charlady while he took the main part, the script dictating that he spent a good deal of the evening writhing about in greying underpants on the grass stage. Deep down, my no-nonsense self thought him a drip for such self-indulgence. And when, later, he involved me in improvisation workshops, I suffered the mix of derision and fear which is such a familiar response in me today. The only advantage in taking part was that no lines had to be learnt.

After one such occasion, my important boyfriend's friend, a vividly ugly boy who was also extremely attractive and is now well-known in theatrical circles, walked along beside him. They were, as on most days, moving in the direction of a pub. The ugly boy had a scholar girlfriend with china-clear skin, whose sanity seemed always to be in question. I was attracted to her brilliance and her volatility. Indeed, I wanted to be her, just as I wanted to be the girl whom Nick had in tow, for I resented what others envied about me – the stability of my rural upbringing which was to blame for my mundane appearance, and all that I felt I lacked as a person. I wished I could tell the world that I lived in a council flat in Brixton. Failing that, why not be rakish? Announce that I came from Islington or

Wimbledon, which was where Chantal lived, her kitchen table graced always with French cheeses and fruit bowls that send one casting about for a drawing pad.

I still hold a clear image of those two boys walking down the street beside Blackwell's Bookshop, the ugly boy loping along with his hand held out, as if searching for the hand of his scholar Love, whom he eventually married.

One of the chief torments of Oxford was Anglo Saxon. I never understood it, and worked at it as little as possible. *The Battle of Maldon*, *Beowulf*, *The Seafarer* and *The Wayfarer* were all learnt from a yellow book still in my bookcase, alongside my copy of Balzac's *Le Père Goriot*. For books one has had to live with for long spells should surely be treasured.

A.N. Wilson, a young man then, though old of soul, pretended to teach Anglo Saxon. He pointed us to a translation which we learnt by heart in order to avoid the complications of grammar. Now famous, he had all the right ideas about what to do at Oxford – mix with the eminent, find a girlfriend and write a good book. He saved a great deal of time by writing 'very good' at the end of all essays, which they generally were, thanks to having been copied from a book in The Bodleian. But soon, he floated off and we were handed over to a woman who was serious, intense and focused maniacally on declensions and cases. She was depressing to look upon: grey hair scraped back from a plain face into a thin ponytail. In tutorial after tutorial she quoted, evaluated and analysed whole swathes of Anglo-Saxon she recited by heart.

One summer, while on a bench in the garden at Yarde, I found out by some means that our teacher had committed suicide. It was then that I saw what a strain it must have been to teach us; perhaps the effort had even wrung from her the last of her strength. We didn't know her well, but were devastated by the term 'suicide'. It seemed unfair that a person who worked so hard and taught with such generosity should reach such a state of desperation.

It was at this point that my mother, the observing presence in my life, began to worry. Seated on the lawn a yard or so away from the well where we drew our bath water during the drought of 1976, she stared at a paint stain on the path left by my efforts to re-brand my bicycle. Then said in her best WI voice: 'I'm not at all sure that Oxford is the right place for you.' I retorted that of course it was and it was none of her business anyway, in much the same tone as I had denied her information on the status of my virginity only three years earlier. But she was right; Oxford wasn't. Indeed, Oxford became more and more wrong as the second year progressed, culminating in a trip to Egypt: 'You should never have gone to Egypt. Or to Oxford. I'm very cross.' Words unsaid but silently conveyed.

And she was right about Egypt too. There are places to which one shouldn't go; places which do not fit with one's nature. Can do irreparable damage to one's balance and sanity, leading someone like Blanche Dubois – I'm a minority fan – to an asylum.

Or a nunnery.

For the occasion of my flight into Egypt, I had my hair cut into a crew. My mother snapped, 'Why did you do that? You look awful. Just before your sister's wedding! You should have thought. Bridesmaids have long hair. I call that typical of you!'

'Okay, okay…'

And she smacked my head in the way mothers of that generation could smack and be angry and it be understood that you deserved it because the only thing you think about is yourself. Yet, in the photos, my face is young and open. Is a page-boy hairstyle not enough to accompany a bride? My dear sister's wedding photos were taken in the orchard, near the pigsties. I had once tried to colonise those and turn them into a house of my own, using cast-off furniture from my bedroom.

The marquee was put up on the bumpy front lawn. 'We'll have to cut the apple tree down or the marquee won't go up.' I imagine that was what was said, because on my return from Egypt it had gone.

The boy I went to Egypt with – let's call him Frank – wasn't a boyfriend, just a friend. Like most boys I met at Oxford, he was in love with one of my friends who, measured objectively, was the most beautiful of them all. My own boyfriend of the time, he of the greying underpants, who impersonated tortured prisoners and then subjected me to improvisation workshops, was busy doing something else for the summer weeks, and so Frank and I set off. I was in a heightened mood of love; Frank was sombre.

Perhaps our mutual preoccupations were to blame for our casual approach to planning the trip. The extent of our efforts amounted only to a brief glance at a map while seated on high stools in his kitchen the night before departure. Nothing remains of how we went about booking tickets, packing, leaving, saying goodbye to parents… Nothing about the flight remains either.

Cairo, however, is still vivid. It feels now as though we didn't arrive at an airport but landed, ready-dressed in galabeyas, wandering for hours along a road in search of food. All the way, misery consumed me. The place stank of drains; the roads were full of potholes, and everywhere we looked there were vast cones of meat revolving on skewers. When not in the galabeya, I was in pink dungarees – the same I had worn when the Australian boys who kissed me so kindly in Adelaide had visited me in Oxford, rightly expecting a hearty welcome. I was busy at the time – at that delicate stage of an essay when only silence will engender the last point in an argument. They must have thought me ungracious and changed. For gone were the curves and clear skin. Instead – spots, eyebags and other unpleasant small ailments, brought on by neglect and anxious attempts at study.

Everything was a mess in Oxford and my body shouted it out loud. Perhaps this was another reason why we had made no sensible plans. In their stead, a lethal force took over.

My few, indelible memories of Egypt still summon a shiver. We met an American guy with whom we spent two or three days discussing the end of the world, along with his boyfriend. The notion of the world ending had already held a place in my consciousness. Influenced by the politics of the time, my boyfriend in the greying underpants had the same belief: that as a race we wouldn't be around for long. I lived with that conviction between the ages of twenty-two and forty-two.

The pyramids were of moderate interest but, while separated temporarily from Frank, I was chased into a cave by a young Arab. That could have ended badly had I not been a fast runner. Once out of the dark, and standing alone before the Sphinx, I felt small and afraid, as if my solar plexus had been punched.

With the pyramids done, we travelled south to Karnak. The temple itself, in ruins, seemed to stretch endlessly in the white heat. It was almost empty on the day of our visit. I wandered off on my own, only coming to when I bumped into the side of a tomb where there was an isolated splash of red – the only colour for miles, apart from the blue of the sky. It set my head rushing from the age of the pharaohs to a blank stretch of time, in which the present was nothing.

In the days to follow?

We watched feluccas float down the Nile, pretty from a distance. But we were too scared about bilharzia to take a trip on one, or to do anything, apart from return to Cairo.

One late night we found a cheap hotel and were told that there was only room for one guest. Instead of sharing a bed, I told Frank that he should have it, and I would get a taxi to the youth hostel on the edge of town. I have told this story numerous times to children wanting real life, rather than the words into which they have to breathe their own life. Perhaps, over the years, I have distorted the truth of this implausible sounding tale. For why would a young man as kind and decent as Frank have exposed me to such danger so late at night?

'Where going?' The peremptory taxi driver.
'The Youth Hostel.' (Shouting.)

The driver opened the passenger door; I climbed in as if he were a guiding parent who would convey me safely to my destination. It should have been a ten-minute journey. Not for this guy. He was very far from being a parent. On and on he chugged – over a bridge and into another part of the city, which felt as different from where it should have been as Bromley is from Brompton.

'Where are we?'

No answer.

On, on.

The beginnings of panic. Then boredom. Finally, anger. I was tired and wanted to be at home but on he went, until finally I summoned the gumption to shout: 'Please will you stop!'

And stop he did, pulled up the handbrake, took a knife from his pocket and pointed it at my face.

Terror, calm, silence. Then out of nowhere, the sound of a voice loud in my head: *You are protected*. It was the same voice that I had heard in the headmistress's study at Sherborne, and when I was in bed after offering up my maidenhood, and it was a voice I was to hear a great deal more of in the nunnery. With the gift of confidence it brought, I turned to the driver, looked him in the eye, in exactly the manner we are advised not to do when faced by a raging animal, and said, slow as slow: 'Let Me Out!'

Wearily he stretched across me and unlocked the passenger door.

I remember standing in the potholed road, feeling strangely at peace. In the empty moment, I tried to line up the influences at work: I had been troubled since arrival by a premonition involving the god Anubis. Then there was my guiding protector. Who was that? Had my

Church of England God finally roused himself? Whoever or whatever it was, I had been restored to safety.

But where to go so late at night?

No answer.

Just as I feel today at the end of a troubling marriage as if I am standing in the middle of a busy road unable to move, I stood then, and waited. For how long I have no idea; the knife had cut across time in the same way the temple in Karnak had cut across time. Perhaps ten minutes later, fifteen, half an hour, a car with supernaturally bright lights sped towards me, a window was lowered, and a voice called out.

'Are you lost?'

'Yes.'

'Get in.'

Out of one dangerous car and into another. Was I mad? Or was it because there were children in the back, and the remains of party food on the seat. In the warmth of their company, I had another odd feeling – that the voice which had told me I was protected wasn't English at all but Indian. And now I was being rescued by a family from that same country.

It turned out we were miles from the youth hostel.

'It's no problem, we'll take you there, don't worry.'

The hostel closed at midnight. How did I know the time? I never wore a watch; wouldn't and won't, even now. Whatever the case, the driver seemed to know and moved at cosmic speed. In seconds, we arrived at a building where a small man stood, barely visible in the darkness, fiddling with a bunch of keys. I flew out of the car, pleading.

'No, no! Please. Let me in.'

And, as if he too had taken pause for peace, he smiled, unlocked the door and showed me to a room. There I wrapped myself in a grey blanket on a top bunk, shaking, suddenly aware that I had had a close shave with the grim reaper.

The next day, back with Frank in the middle of Cairo, I burst into tears, announced that I hated Egypt and wanted to go home. So that's what we did – packed up and left.

I returned to Devon to be met by my mother, cross with my Buddhist haircut and flustered over the arrangements for my sister's wedding.

I shall never forget the fresh taste of Devonshire water.

'THE LUNATICS'

(2)

Summer 1978.

It was the middle of the night. A hand, dry and callused, shot out and slapped itself into mine. I was asleep but I am wide awake now. And feel I have been ever since. Not a single night's unbroken sleep, for over forty years…

His wife writes.

His friend writes.

Both of them tell me that he saw this encounter of hands as the start of his period of psychosis. As for me, it marked the beginning of my departure from life itself.

Let's begin that again.

Rationally.

My second year at Oxford and I was acting in another play. In the early rehearsals the two of us, players in a drama that was as much cosmic as theatrical, barely exchanged a word. But something was happening between us as if, in an echo from the past, it could be heard only between the words of casual conversation. A look – a sense – felt in the body and deep in the mind, a memory stirring. And then that slap of the hand, which occurred because Nick, the director, announced that the cast were to live together for a week, in a house in Summertown: 'So you can get into your parts.' As usual, I was vague about the play's plot and could barely remember my lines. Thankfully, they were few while he had whole swathes.

But why was he on the bed and me on the floor? Let's blame Ann Wordsworth. Everything is usefully pinned upon her hunched but influential, feminist shoulders which broke into pieces all that I had ever understood about how a good life works.

Both of us are asleep. Little snuffles issue from other members of the cast in the room. Then suddenly we are wide awake, the air full of an emotion so charged I am shaking. Out shoots my arm in the darkness. And there is Oliver's arm, then his hand smacking hard into mine.

That was that. Our fate was sealed. Or mine was, at least, for in that clasping of hands, lay the beginning of my departure from life itself. Those words, at least, bear repeating.

Oliver was intelligent and well-connected. He knew all the most talented people in Oxford and was on first name terms with his tutor, who later reviewed his poetry. He had no need of a Mr Brown; he was his own Mr Brown. He wasn't loud and moneyed like Quentin, gadding about in a cloak, but modest and deep and admired. He also had an artist sister who soon became in some way a component of our liaison, mythologised I see now.

For much of the time that I knew him, Oliver wore a maroon embroidered jacket. Like my father, he had sloping shoulders and was, in many ways, more like a girl than a boy. His favourite writer was D.H. Lawrence and he went through a period when he thought he was the reincarnation of Lawrence. He did indeed bear an uncanny resemblance, though he shared neither Lawrence's beard nor his height.

For my part, Lawrence had remained unexplored; novels too long, too repetitive, though I got through *The Rainbow* one summer many years later, without moving from my bed by the window in a cottage in Kent. What I longed for then was answers and good grades. Now, books and their writers are my dearest solace.

One holiday, when I went to stay with Oliver's parents, who lived in a small modern house that my parents would have disapproved of, we walked the length of a day enjoying Hoshi-like conversations, lying in a wood to form the shape of a heart with our bodies. Once, we made love in a wood. The ground, crawling with insects, wasn't conducive to the ease of mind that act at its loveliest can lead to. But now I am glad to think of the earth bringing us down to its grubby self. A contrast, then, with the lofty ideals we aspired to when fixated on Wordsworth, Coleridge, Keats...

At the outset of our love, I spent time with Oliver in his grand college rooms. The first time, we slept like orphans on the floor. In fact, there was an orphan-like quality to our love throughout. I wore his black V-neck jumper and with great care, the same care with which he did everything. One evening, he placed a vinyl record on his turntable and out came the words the psychometrist of Oxford market had spoken.

Tears of sorrow and tears of joy.

A shudder went through me, as if, alongside the rightness in finding him, there also lay danger.

Another day, an occasion which rang with significance, we were walking over Magdalen Bridge when Oliver turned to me and said, 'Let's go into this church.'

We sat side by side in a dark pew, he swivelling round to stare into my eyes. Then, in a hushed voice, he announced that we were going to change the world; that we were Jesus and Mary, or that he was Jesus and I was his disciple.

'You didn't actually believe that, did you?' people ask me now. Yes, I did believe it, feeling that he was on to something that wasn't provided by our academic studies – a sense of having a part to play in the world's story.

That summer we took the train to Inverness and slept in a bed and breakfast between bri-nylon sheets, where we indulged in a slow, captivating form of love-making that seemed more spiritual than physical. In fact, the most physical thing about it came afterwards when together, me in a red hand-knitted jumper and jeans, we went to a pub for bangers and mash and enjoyed an obnoxious sense of superiority over the loud men at the bar whose voices we mimicked.

The next day, Oliver's thoughts with the Celts and Wordsworth, mine with Oliver and a stomach ache, we took a small train to the Kyle of Lochalsh and walked in the hills and pouring rain. A fog formed and, by the time it had cleared, it was too late to turn back and the danger became part of the excitement. We aimed, it seemed always, for the edge, but slowly and methodically, as if, in observing the subtlety of things, we might pass through some barrier and arrive in another world.

As we staggered in the half dark down a steep hillside, a bothy came into sight. Inside, food had been left by other travellers; we also had small packets of dried edibles that Oliver cooked with the skill of a seasoned camper. On what? A homemade fire? Inside the bothy? Outside the bothy? There was a zealousness to Oliver's approach, as if he was imitating the poet Edward Thomas, that expert at map reading and survival skills who is now so admired that hardly a scholar dare write of him.

Early the next morning, we bathed naked in an ice-cold stream then walked on. Or stayed another night? Either way, this was no ordinary trip. There was something else going on, above, around or within us, which made our love-making in a sleeping bag feel like, a forewarning...

Sometime during the following term, Oliver announced that we must visit a friend of his who had a message to give us.

The friend had oversized buck teeth which looked as if they might wobble. But Oliver considered him special, and it is true that sitting in his rooms which, in my spatially-unaware mind, comes to me now as being somewhere on the left-hand side of a courtyard, the air fell heavily silent – that dense silence which seemed to be everywhere Oliver went. Casting small talk aside, the friend, a fan of

Anglo Saxon and ancient Norse literature, announced, 'We've all three met before in another life – in China.' The atmosphere instantly became weighted and deep, ringing with a truth that I have found in no person or place since. For everyone I have ever met since (other than my fellow nuns) has stated with certainty that reincarnation is a self-regarding myth.

The writer Hanif Kureishi claimed, when divulging his inner life to the psychiatrist Dr Anthony Clare, that it's absurd to think of yourself as a 'fixed entity. That is a fiction we turn to in times of trouble.' Perhaps Kureishi was one of Ann Wordsworth's students? He'd be about the right age.

Oliver and I, on the other hand, were certain that there was a soul. In honour of that conviction, which accorded with my childhood sense of individuality that Marxism had so challenged, there came a time when we and his buck-toothed friend began spending our evenings in a rented house in the south of the city, meditating. We followed no set method for this practice, and quite soon felt we were dabbling with forces beyond our understanding. It was at this moment that my childhood self reared its head. What it asserted was that we would get as lost as I had got lost in Ann Wordsworth's shed for, in our obscure practice, we seemed to enter a great space in which there was nothing but silence and a chilly breeze.

One evening, Oliver's friend leant backwards in his grubby armchair, head against an antimacassar, and slipped into a trance. After ten minutes, he returned to our presence bearing messages. It was unclear from whence they came – but aliens were mentioned. While my Devon self, more used to boats and sausages, was beginning to object to the extremes of such other-worldly dabblings, I did remain intrigued, for I was Mary, or a disciple, and Oliver was Jesus. And so of course the message must be important and might usefully excuse me therefore from any further academic work.

Perhaps my stubborn scepticism had something to do with the mundane quality of the words from beyond that were intended for me. Having been told by the psychometric to eat my vegetables sitting down, and focus mainly on broccoli ('Kofi Annan'), now I was instructed to cut down on sugar. Then came the words I have often tried since to unpick.

There is a full story above the kitchen.

The relationship with Oliver ended because…

Why? Why did it end? And how? Was it me? Him? All that is clear is that once it was over I felt that I had lost the greater part of myself.

At some point in the months after graduation, Oliver wrote me a reprimanding letter: he asserted that I was the sort of person who would either fully embrace a spiritual life or become debauched. Either way, I would never find a balance between pleasure and purpose – in other words, I would go mad. This hurt, for there is certainly a truth to it, as my sequel to this story will reveal.

Even when we were together, Oliver didn't seem to see himself suffering the same fate. Indeed, while still at

Oxford, and living in a rented room, he claimed to have been visited in a dream by a girl with long black hair, floating above a bright blue sea. Later, he married her lookalike. She was pretty and played the flute. Either by chance or fate's cruel finger, she taught maths at the same school where I began my own teaching career. Tearing at my heart, Oliver came to that school once. He came again to my second school, where my head of department invited him to conduct a workshop of some kind, for it turned out he had taught him English at secondary school.

By that time I was a fully-fledged nun, and so terrified was I of my buried feelings of love that when Oliver appeared, I made sure my head of department walked between us, as if we were two children on either side of a stern parent.

Since those days, forty or so years ago, I have dreamt many times of Oliver. On each occasion I wake in distress, for the dreams seem always to involve an element of competition. Also, something else I cannot identify, for it has been a year or so since he has been a part of my night. I have dreamt of Oxford too: of being back there, but not knowing anyone and having no idea whether I am student or visitor.

Indeed, I often wake not knowing what room I am sleeping in. My eyes are open, I can see the blue and white dressing table I bought with the money my parents left me in their will, but I still have no idea where I am. And soon I am to move from this house and will be in another strange environment, as yet unknown.

Divorced. Maybe dead. Or so it feels today.

THE SEEKER

Oliver did well in his finals. For many years, I was sure he'd taken a first as he had in his Honour Moderations. But after my father died, I found, stuffed inside a bible that served as his filing cabinet, a yellowing newspaper cutting listing our results. I gained an upper second. So did he.

But the question was, what to do with that second? Where to go? Oxford had had its fill of us and we of each other. So, in the end that has no end, I returned exhausted, by train, to Yarde, dragging twenty or so carrier bags beside me.

My father: 'What's all that lot?'

'Wherever you go you make a mess.' (My mother.)

It was tiredness.

And it was still tiredness whenever I trailed around the school that I have thankfully retired from, carrying all that I had taken home the previous night only to return it for another ten hours's trekking from one classroom to another. Dyspraxia/ADHD were conditions not recognised when I was a child, while perhaps both are revealed by my propensity for carrying unnecessary luggage around.

The period post-Oxford was particularly unpleasant. I was afflicted with stomach pains so severe that I looked as if I was pregnant with triplets. Over the months, the pain became worse, the phantom pregnancy more visible. Not the kind of condition one talks about to parents. For in those days, before the aches and pains of their own old age set in, they only understood measles or pneumonia, at least a formally labelled ailment. Had it been an actual pregnancy, it is best left unimagined how they might have reacted.

That summer, a naturopath with beautiful skin and a turban came to live in our South Devon village. She was from the breed of woman my parents thought 'weird', so I kept my appointment a secret – as I usually do among people who prefer not to disturb convention.

'Come upstairs please and lie down. In here.'

'In here' was her bedroom and where I was to recline on a bed, single and counterpaned. I had expected a doctor's surgery and waiting room, for deep down I was, then, just as conventional as my parents.

'Well,' the woman said through her floppy lips, her currant-bun hand on my tummy. 'There's no pulse. Or next to none.'

'What does that mean?'

'Just what I've said: little or no pulse.' She could have been kinder, I felt, given she was going to charge a fee.

'What do I do about that?'

'Change your diet.'

'How? What do I eat?'

'You are never again in your life to eat meat, or the pulse in your stomach will stop for good,' she snapped.

'Then what will happen?'

'You'll die.'

I was a little shocked, for I was quite ready to be told that my problem was psychosomatic. She supplied me with some mushrooms, such as you see in the windows of Chinese medicine shops. These I was to boil up in water on the Aga. Then there were pills and a diet sheet, which included several cups of camomile tea a day, and at least three bowls of lentils a week washed down with miso soup.

At first, my mother, busy queening around the village in one of her hats, took no notice. After all, I was twenty-one and had the right to eat what I liked. And I found myself a job – in Harris's Bacon Factory in Totnes.

'It was all because of that factory,' my parents came to say. 'That's what made you become so peculiar.'

The situation came to a head one Sunday lunchtime.

'What's wrong with you? Lovely piece of pork. You love crackling. Come on.'

'I'm having lentils.'

The air went dark.

Within three weeks my whole body was relieved, pleased, no longer ached. My mother thought otherwise. So livid was she that, after lunch one day, she marched to the naturopath's house – a cottage on the corner of our orchard – and registered her displeasure. 'We live at the heart of the village – have been here for years and years and you've just arrived from Japan of all places to interfere in our lives' was the gist of her statement. I hope she worded it more euphemistically.

The next time I met 'that menace of a quack whoever she is', the naturopath was extremely brisk, unpleasant even, telling me that my mother had been rude to her. I wasn't surprised – my mother's inner tiger manifested itself about four times a year. 'You have corrupted my daughter. You've made her ill. She looks awful. What have you done to her? And who and what are you anyway?'

The naturopath had helped me feel better. This involved losing weight, which was bound to happen after cutting out the fatty foods.

But the sadness was that I was emotionally lost. My parents seemed a million miles away, for they had never read Harold Bloom or Roland Barthes. I am ashamed now that I thought them intellectually inferior. They were good, simple people, not stupid at all, and perhaps not even so simple either.

The job at Harris's Bacon Factory, a temporary measure against lostness, seemed to everyone in the family cruelly ironic. It was half a mile outside Totnes. Arriving there on time meant rising at seven to wolf down the naturopath's prescribed cereal, which tasted like flapjacks; then make a wholemeal picnic lunch and a flask of camomile tea. I would bolt up the hill to meet Mr Hill, a man from the village who also worked in Totnes, and we would set off in his van. I delighted in the drive through rounded swathes of brick-red farmland, while he talked in his broad Devon accent then dropped me outside the factory (now converted into a block of high-end flats), with never so much as a mention of money from him or a thank you from me.

I clocked in, donned a white coat and lace bath hat and spent the day standing opposite a woman called Ivy, injecting freshly baked pork pies with gelatine – an unexpectedly pleasant experience. The squeals and bellows from the abattoir, so horribly close to the wholesome process of baking, caused me no alarm. I had been brought up on a farm, after all; had been shown how to wring a chicken's neck before I was ten. So that wasn't the problem. It was deeper than that. More vital.

What on earth was I to do with my life?

'What we think you should do is a course in something practical.'

'Why?'

'Because then you can get a job until you've decided what you really want to do.'

'So, you're sending me away again.'

'We're not sending you away. We just think you need a practical qualification.'

But they were sending me away again. This time to London, to live with my brother, who was training to be an accountant and living in a lush flat rented from a friend with funds. While he did accounting, I did typing. I drove to Pitman's Secretarial College in Russell Square, on a moped (surely that word should be hyphenated?). How the moped ever found me is a mystery – but it was blue and I was proud of it. Later, when working in Exeter, I drove it too fast and landed on a car bonnet. I have had quite a few mishaps (another word in need of a hyphen) in my life (particularly in August) for no other reason than dyspraxia or anxiety.

I shall lay the blame at the now-buried feet of my Cousin Holly, brave survivor of a Japanese prisoner of war camp, who owned a pale-blue, three-wheeler Reliant Robin in which he taught me to drive. In Devon, he and I would motor around the village, taking much the same route as the chauffeur who had abducted me when I was three. Cousin Holly had no interest in the details of gear-changing, but let me drive on while he opined on the novels of Graham Greene and Somerset Maugham.

Most of the people on the typing course were blonde, beautiful and rich, wore high, brown boots and tweed jackets, and weren't too bothered whether they passed the exams or not. All were female. The typing was particularly difficult because there was no delete button, just a roll of Tipp-Ex that had to be rammed in small white strips between paper and hammer to whiten our errors. The paper tore easily, for it was as flimsy and dull as the subject matter it carried.

Shorthand was satisfying for being beautiful to look at, though I can't use it now. But I can type as fast as a pocket rocket, so the course was worth the four (or was it three?) hundred pounds it cost and the three (or was it four?) months of endurance.

I didn't once participate in London society. Why not? I was still on the lentil diet, my brother disapproving of it as much as my parents did. Thus, it alienated me from him, from the world in general.

After the wide plains of Australia, the beautiful Devon fields, the depth of conversation at Oxford, life of a sudden had contracted into a spiral notepad, a few bags of nuts and the daily ride on the blue moped from Hammersmith to Bloomsbury.

I must have communicated with my dear brother, Tim, in some way, for the next thing that happened was that I was put to work, assisting the father of one of his friends. I can recall the name of neither friend nor father, but enough remains of the weeks I spent with him to recognise that this was seminal among the many passing encounters in my life.

He lived in Topsham, in a tall house overlooking the Exe estuary. Quite bulky, like Quentin, he had a blocked nose. Unlike Quentin, he had crinkled hair and buck teeth. He also wore a dun-coloured macintosh, not unlike that worn by the beloved Mr Brown at my second boarding school. I shouldn't remember the macintosh, given that it was summer when I took up the post. But many years later, when I was living as a nun in London, he found out where I was and came with great kindness to the door to enquire if I was all right. Perhaps it was then that he was wearing his macintosh?

My task was to help him with his ideas by typing them out. Perhaps he thought that, as an Oxford graduate, I'd have some ideas of my own, some know-how at least, in the manner of that charming girl of 'fine features' who assisted Candia McWilliam with her excellent memoir: *What to Look for in Winter*. But know-how is just what I didn't have. In fact, I had nothing. As part of a process of cleansing embarked on the moment I left Oxford, I had stopped reading, stopped listening to music, been to no plays… I cared only to run by the river, think about the universe and eat platefuls of lentils. I also smoked three cigarettes a day, two in the morning, one in the evening.

The job lasted less than three months. My employer soon got wise to my problems with typing and invited me instead to sit in his office, where he would ask what I thought of his latest draft of a scene. He had written a play about a boss's seduction of his secretary. I was a person of no particular opinions, but I knew it wasn't just bad, but grubby.

As soon as the day in his dark house came to a close, I would run home in the second-hand blue dress from Oxford market, my long hair tight in a topknot. I'd pull on a pair of shorts and jog beside the river, so that gradually Oxford, in all its dense detail and dogmatism, seemed to disperse in the fresh air. The pulse in all parts of my body was perking up, eyes brightening, skin glowing, so that my body and I felt as good as ever they had in their combined life.

At the same time there was something very wrong.

It was as if someone had folded me up and put me inside a sealed container. Now and then, I'd walk across the road from Monmouth Street where I lived, sit in a wine bar, smoke my third cigarette and drink a glass of wine. The pleasure would have been helped by some company. And yet I knew, as if an invisible force was guiding me, that friendship in this phase was, for some reason, forbidden.

Things happen. Time passes. By some means, another job was found – Exeter Library. This involved riding my moped into the centre of town, and a daily meeting with a man, beset by dandruff and boredom, who spent his day laying out newspapers and fiddling with card indexes.

'The books beginning with M, N, O are out of order. Sort them out then do some dusting.'

At home, wherever it be, this would have taken up a couple of minutes at most, but here the object was to fill the whole day. I mastered the art of looking busy until just after lunch. It was then that I'd find a shelf, slump against it and fall asleep. It was after one such nap, still a little groggy, having dreamt about a llama drugged on chlorophyll, that I had my moped accident. Fortunately, the driver of the car, on whose bonnet my moped and I had alighted, made very little fuss.

Shortly afterwards, I resigned from the library job. I kept the moped.

I had achieved a classic evader trick a few months earlier in London whilst shop-personning in Selfridges. That job was worse than the library, for I was unwisely assigned to the fabric department. My parents thought this amusing, remembering the many damning reports of my needlework skills at school. And indeed, the task wasn't straightforward.

'I'd like x yards of this please.'

'Right.'

'I said x by y.'

'Yes, I know.'

The roll of green, blue, red fabric had to be balanced on the counter and rapidly unrolled so that it didn't slip to the floor, one edge held parallel to a brass measure. Then, with a huge pair of scissors and a nick, the blade slid in a straight line, material held aloft, shaken, folded, bagged and billed for.

One day, I told my black-suited boss that I didn't feel very well and was going home.

Home then was the minuscule dwelling of an old school friend – she of the apple cheeks and great sweetness whom I had forced into reading to me when I couldn't get to sleep at Sherborne. This time, I was genuinely unwell. Once better, I didn't return to the fabric department, didn't even announce that I was resigning. I just stayed in the house, wore a billowing grey tweed skirt and a green mohair tank top, and entertained a German baron I had vaguely dated towards the end of my time at Oxford. He was a tall man who played classical guitar and lived in Bonn. How he knew I was in London, or what we had to do with each other by then, is lost in time. But he reappeared in a recent news item, detailing, whether reliably or not I don't know, that his father had been in the bunker with Hitler when he (Hitler) had committed suicide.

There were two other jobs that came to fill my pre- and post-graduate limbo. The Lotus Pottery belonged to our next-door neighbour, a potter himself, with ginger hair and sideburns, who wore red canvas trousers. That, too, was a dull job involving dusting pots, moving pots from one shelf to another, talking about pots, selling pots, wrapping pots, ad infinitum.

To protect my brain from premature decay, I didn't read Dostoevsky, Gertrude Stein, Chomsky... Instead, I knitted an ivory scarf in acrylic, deciding from the start that it should be made as long as the time on the job afforded. It turned out to be a very long scarf, and was never worn, though it might have made a good stair runner.

I left the pottery as soon as I could without being rude, which was harder than leaving Selfridges because it was important for my parents to be on good terms with their neighbours. The pottery slowed the pulse in my stomach. As did working in the village hotel under a man who was sinister, in a friendly kind of way, as every owner of that hotel seemed to have been.

For a period during our youth, my parents rented out their spare room, to help out the hotel owner, Mr Fox, when he had run out of space. One day, when they were out, Mr Fox came to introduce his overflow guests to Yarde. Finding the house locked, he fetched a ladder, climbed through a window, and unlocked the house from inside in order to show his guests to their room. At this break-in, my mother was livid. But she had to pretend she didn't mind for she was in the habit of taking yoga lessons with Mrs Fox, free of charge. My father considered Mrs Fox vulgar because she wore a kaftan and bejewelled mules.

Under the sinister proprietor, I worked as a chambermaid, alongside a woman called Ivy, who might well have been the same Ivy who later helped me inject gelatine into Harris's pork pies.

The best thing about both the pottery and the hotel was the fact that all workers stopped for elevenses at ten-thirty. My parents synchronised at home, also entertaining Lulu, our family's other mother, who brought a breeze of joy into a house that was, in some way, sad. The mere sound of Lulu's voice, her warm Devon vowels, banished all darkness. And when in a nursing home from where she recently died, she was said to be the lady of the house, for her high-spirited talk was never to be silenced.

Cousin Holly, my beloved driving instructor, was also there. For, after his wife had died, he'd moved to Stoke Gabriel from Buckfastleigh, and always came for elevenses. Invariably he would bear the gift of an old book, on the inside covers of which he'd written in tiny script all relevant facts about the life of the writer, with a particular focus on military detail.

He, too, died in a home in his late eighties. My mother visited him once a week for several years. And she spent much of her fifth decade nobly advising those who mismanaged homes for the elderly.

It would have been later, at one of these protracted morning coffee sessions that I enjoyed regaling my parents with the inside news of the village hotel. They were avid listeners, latching in particular onto a story about the misfortunes of one elderly male guest.

'Yesterday,' I began, 'when Ivy and I were making the beds, we went into this room with the cleaning trolley, thinking it would be empty and then this bloke's head ('Don't say bloke') stuck up from the other side of the bed.'

'I call that stupid!'

'No, listen! Then his head told me to fetch his legs. Then Ivy fainted and I ran round to look and there was this small torso balanced on the floor, the hand of one arm, pointing to the cupboard. So, I opened the cupboard and two really long legs were propped diagonally inside.'

He said: 'Yes, those. Bring them here. Please.'

'Here' also meant: 'Please revive your fainting friend and leave the room so that I can get up in privacy.'

'And then guess what, Mummy listen, we went out

into the corridor, Ivy had recovered and we saw this really tall guy who must have been the legless man ('Don't say guy!') walking nonchalantly along the corridor.'

My parents were tickled, but what I wanted to know was how the man had got his legs into the cupboard the night before and then himself into bed. Where was his wife? For in my then-world, all men had wives and all wives helped their men to do things that they couldn't do for themselves.

The story enjoyed a long lease of life, within my father's sparse conversation, just as my mother often recounted my childhood dream of the man with the gun tied to a washing-up bottle. I recall no mention of the war, which is surely where the man/bloke/gentleman had been separated from his legs.

Why did my parents make so much of my sickening enthusiasm? Perhaps they were bored, perhaps proud; perhaps it was their way of showing love? It was certainly their way of demonstrating that life should be fun and that it was no good being down in the mouth, too cold, too hot, homesick, negative or inferior. Nor, to add to an earlier list, should one be loud, brash, wear bright colours, have a regional accent, say 'pardon' or 'lounge' or 'toilet' or 'afters', or have one's nose pierced, arms tattooed (unless in the merchant navy), and so on and so on... The code of that loveable, secure, blinkered culture that has died with them.

When they were elderly, however, because they came to rely on those very people with tattoos and piercings and mispronunciations to help them in and out of the bath, the loo, the world, my parents became soft at the centre as well as brittle, delicate and charming.

When it was suggested that Yarde was too big and, without putting it explicitly that way, that over decades of neglect they had let it fall into disrepair, my father's reaction was to return to his chair by the fire. There he lit his pipe, spaniels at his feet, and stayed shtum. My brother and sister and I, meanwhile, sat in the kitchen at the square formica table, gently conversing with our mother, trying to convince her that the house was too much hard work and they needed more help. Thus was set in motion the monumental move from a farmhouse to a modern bungalow on the outskirts of the village.

My parents had always been as rude about bungalows as they were about caravans. In fact, there was not much they weren't rude about in their time. Anything to do with taking tablets they particularly despised, though it was during, or perhaps even before, the big move that they began their own drug-taking routines, piling up prescriptions and going together to the doctor's surgery for various small indignities.

It was painful watching these two dear stoics surrender to frailties they had so long derided; agony, in fact, to see the stiffness go from their upper lips. Watching them move house was particularly poignant. My father did nothing; my mother made lists. Of what to do with this, that and every tiny other: the books, the china, the pictures, the clothes, the old suitcases, the old everything. She was admirably methodical. But on a visit from home in Kent back to Devon, I was sad to find her sleeping in a room on her own and asking for a cup of warm milk to be brought 'at about three in the morning to help me sleep', as well as a collection of children's books with happy endings.

'I only want to read stories to do with families,' she said. 'Not your kind of books – nothing dark or spiritual.'

THE DRIFTER

When I walked out on the writer in Topsham, then the library, and another dreary typing job on an industrial estate just outside Exeter, I felt so far from any sense of belonging that I applied for a place on a teaching course in Birmingham, a city chosen only for its being as different from Oxford as Hove is from Halifax.

Acceptance on the course involved an interview, for which I wore my long-serving, cornflower-blue dress bought in Oxford market. By this point, I was looking unwell. But I was an Oxford graduate and this was the first year of the course, so the interviewer accepted me, along with a group of eight or so others who have probably long turned out to be productive members of society with solid careers behind them and a proud batch of productive offspring.

The feeling of estrangement from this kind of conventional life hadn't been helped by a visit to Yarde. Topsham to Stoke Gabriel is about thirty miles so I hitched a lift, an acceptable method of travel in the late seventies. Being distracted, I didn't notice that the man who pulled up was wearing no clothes. So, here was France all over again. But this time on wheels and no escape.

Why did I get into the car? I had enjoyed no sexual

encounters of note since Oliver; perhaps this hiatus had made me unobservant of physical detail?

Inside the car, door shut, nakedness noted, I sat bolt upright, bag on lap, eyes forward like the prim schoolmistress I was later not to become.

The nudist, who was something akin to an unpleasantly smelling mussel, its hand – tentacle – clamped over its crotch, suddenly provoked desperate thoughts: is he wearing a seat belt, is his car an automatic, is there anything in my bag heavy enough to make his eyes water with a wop to his vitals? No such measure was necessary. He simply drove all the way to Torquay.

'Goodbye.'

'Thanks for the ride.'

'No problem. I'm going to the beach.'

And he opened the door, with only the faintest of brushes against my bare arm.

I don't remember how I found my way from Torquay to Stoke Gabriel.

What I do recall is saddening, though it must be familiar to what so many of us experience when returning to our childhood homes. For talking to my parents was like a communication with strangers.

I turned once more to my faithful and angst-free friend, Loo Brown, who was living alone, doing nothing very much in a cottage on the edge of Exeter. She was, it now seems to me, always happy doing nothing, but she was also capable of very hard work. Only recently she retired from running a busy wholefood restaurant in Crediton where she never took days off.

In a rented cottage, at the bottom of a winding lane, Loo, who had also just left university, was happy chopping logs, stoking an open fire, pottering... The meaning of life, God, the reader, the writer, the critic seemed far from her mind. But I have met her again over thirty years later, and recognised in her an unarticulated depth in whose space she must, in those young days, have instinctively found her rest. I took refuge with her for what must have been weeks, months, while continuing to pay rent for the shared cottage in Topsham. Did I contribute financially? Did I buy food? I fear I didn't, instead taking it as given that I would be accepted for nothing. None of us Church children were taught to talk about the correct exchange of money.

After a while, I found myself floating in the blue dress, back to the cottage in Topsham, which I shared with a strong, hockey-playing Australian. We had nothing in common. We slept in adjacent rooms, mine quite large, with a mattress on the floor, my few second-hand clothes strewn about and, always close by, the white silk dressing gown my brother had brought me from Hong Kong. Its flimsy lightness most aptly represented the very slight figure I had become.

Because I didn't want to be here...

LAST STEPS

After university, my most sustaining activity was jogging. I returned to it again when living in London and, more recently, in Kent. It was a tactic precious to an evader the day before a friend's funeral, the day after teaching badly, teaching too well, falling in love...

But then, jobless in Topsham before my teaching course in Birmingham began, I was like someone with no feet at all. So that one day, I stopped.

No more running.

Came to a standstill, mind suddenly without shape or form as if washed of all thought. I ate without pleasure; drank wine without pleasure. An addict by nature, perhaps I added a fourth cigarette to my daily ration of three? The pulse in my stomach, happy only with purpose, spluttered once more to a halt. Details have blurred. Only the sorrow – no, not sorrow, for sorrow is keen and sharp. This was a feeling of endlessness, like being in a cloud, but not soft.

Looking back, from another strange phase – the end of a marriage and a career – I see how terrified and untrusting I was. Life stretched before my young body, but without any discernible route: no story to write of it, no choreography to dance to it, no school, no teacher to help shape and correct it. But there was instinct of a kind.

Instinct had brought me to this state of emptiness, as if it knew that what was to come would require a purity so total that I would fall into it lightly, completely and without resistance.

First, to walk. One day to take a walk. No direction, no reason. Down lanes, through built-up areas, into the deep of the countryside in search of a meadow. There, I stopped, stared up at a wide sky, the air thin and white, and me with it. And, suddenly, as if from nowhere, a thought shot through me with the force and velocity of a bullet.

Okay, then. If you're there. If you want me to do something. This is your moment.

FIND ME!

I had been brought up on convictions, taught to take a stand. But not once, before or since, was a stand for myself made – yelled – screamed with such force.

My family: 'That was the end really, wasn't it. You never really lived after that, did you!'

'That's not true! I lived more then than at any time in my life.'

What I didn't tell them was that one of the first instructions issued to me as a nun was that I was to 'die alive'.

The perfect solution!

'It didn't look like it to us.'

Whatever they thought, felt, said, the shock waves that followed, not the answer, but my own plea, stayed with me for three days.

Routine fell to nothing.

I remained as much as possible, like my father alone in his chair, waiting.

As now I wait too.

For I knew that if I took a step I would fall.

'Well, you did fall, didn't you, after that.'

'I don't think so.'

'Of course you did. They always get a person when they're vulnerable.'

'It didn't feel like that. It felt like a preparation.'

'That's not how it looked to us.'

To me now, to them, us, whoever… it doesn't matter. For the answer to my moment in the meadow came surely and clearly…

The nunnery.

And the nunnery which found me, not in Devon but Edinburgh, held me in its arms for twenty long years, stretching like a road through my child-bearing years and into middle age; a life that was as different from family life as a meadow from a prison.

Of how it happened, and where and what occurred during it, another time. For that life of enclosure and intensity belongs apart from that which led up to it and that, too, which led away from it.

I shall name it: *Out of This World*.

ACKNOWLEDGEMENTS

Ian Anderson, Flo Bender, Loo Brown, Sheila Brownlee, Aidan Chambers, Andy Dixon, Katie Glenville, Alan Granley, Frances Hedgeland, Neville Hodgkinson, Emma Innes, Kathryn Lloyd, John Merivale, Robert Nurden, Eugene Romain, John Seal, Alison Shakspeare, David Whitley, the peace of Strawberry Hill House.

www.ingramcontent.com/pod-product-compliance
Ingram Content Group UK Ltd.
Pitfield, Milton Keynes, MK11 3LW, UK
UKHW011833050625
6245UKWH00002B/156